Introduction

Sayings and linguistic expressions tell us a lot about people and their verbal habits. In Nova Scotia, with its old traditions and time-honoured way of life, people speak an interesting mixture acquired from various cultures, professions, and geographical locations. The earliest peoples with their unique cultures including the Mi'kmaq, Acadians, Scots, Blacks, English, and Irish, have all contributed to our rich use of language. And many writers have mined this great regional lexicography down through the centuries including Thomas Chandler Haliburton, Helen Creighton, Clara Dennis, Marion Robertson, Thomas H. Raddall, and more recently, Lewis Poteet, Mike Parker, and Clary Croft. Another major influence on this linguistic development has been the diverse ways Nova Scotians earn a living whether from the sea, the woodland, or from the soil itself. Those who grew up around the sea certainly came to speak a different assortment of phrases and expressions than those who lived inland.

In gathering this collection, I was struck with the astonishing number of colourful and intriguing phrases that come from the sea, both the nautical experiences of building and sailing ships around the globe, and the extensive linguistic customs and traditions Nova Scotians have developed around the fishery. While a similar book about New Brunswick's odd use of language yielded a huge inventory of interesting phrases from the lumber industry, Nova Scotia's immense relationship with all aspects of the sea is front and center in this collection. So many phrases immediately jump out such as I spoke him, Joner, labouring oar, laid well, launching day, sixty-four pieces, lay over, the leading line and the leading wind, wedge up, knock down dogs, shachly blocks, pile on the canvas, and "the wood ain't growin' yet that'll beat Bluenose."

Fishing expressions are also rich and colourful, perhaps because fishermen have downtime at sea when they can dream up unusual sayings and phrases. For example, there's Novies and Yanks, banker and barbells, nippers and wristers, dryfoot and hangshore, bloaters, headers, and the bow net, dressing crew, and flying set, mess shad and on count, fish on the half-line, and they were nailin' cod to the masts. And what about sound advice from fishermen such as "better a small fish than an empty dish" or "wind is in the west, fishing will be the best." The list is fascinating and goes on and on.

Beside the fishery and the sea, Nova Scotians have had a long tradition harvesting timber in the back lots and this tradition has given rise to many interesting expressions including cuttin' and fallin,' when she's payin,' snouted it, tending out, striker, log'em and stog'em, ten dollars a thousand, fifty for a thousand, and in the Mersey woods. Farming is one of our oldest occupations and plenty of slang has built up around this historic way of life such as orts and otts, between hay and grass, cow's milk, tramp the mow, make it to the grass, barn raising, yaffle, whip-handle tree, and sidehill farm. Coal mining in northern Nova Scotia and in Cape Breton occurred almost as soon as the first settlers arrived, and the use of language in this occupation is especially vibrant. Some examples include black lung, bump, coalin' up, donkey engine, duff, dummy walls, bob-tailed sheet, fleeting, gob, gundy hole, in the pit, and mucking. For one hundred years, Nova Scotia was a major steel producing province and this industry gave rise to countless distinctive terms and phrases including break, mudding, and pickup, Bloody Sunday, bundling bed, melter, scarfing, slag, and the tar ponds.

Other areas where priceless phrases and odd language took hold include celebrations; gladders, window parties, real cocker, shin-dig, ceilidh, frolic, tore the house down, set the town agog, whisky and fight, and stay out all night, tomfoolery, and the time tonight. Weather lore contributes greatly to our provincial character and some examples include chickens take shelter before rain, freeze the nuts off a brass monkey, fallish, green Christmas white Easter, and at least there's no black flies. Drinking terms of course are everywhere in Nova Scotia and include snapped up, shined up, shit-faced, pour, as cheap as water and a slight more plentiful, dead soldier, drank like a fish, and fell off the wagon. Food phrases – can't find the potatoes for the lobster, Bud the Spud, cadiddles, chow down, cruddy, dandelion greens and fried gaspereau, and a big Dutch mess. Some examples of military terms are A-A for apples, careless talk cost lives, Camp Aldershot, Camp Norway, drank the King's money, eat hash and like it, fart sack, and go easy. Favourite bird nicknames include Alderbird, Black-polls, Bone-knocker, Camp Thief, and fall gull. Colourful language also exists around wild plants and trees such as Canoe Birch, Bec' apple, Cow tongue, monkey birch, and pasture pine. In addition, there are a fair assortment of phrases included here that defy classification but shed plenty of light on Nova Scotians' love of weird and wonderful language such as Bee's knees, first footed, buggers, coosie, and corker.

I have also incorporated a number of odd or distinctive place names due to

The Nova Scotia
Phrase Book

Sayings, Expressions, and Odd Names of Nova Scotia

Dan Soucoup

Maritime Lines

ISBN 1-894420-30-6
ISBN13 978-1-89442030-3
June/07
Maritime Lines
Distribution: Nimbus Publishing
Cover photo: Arthut Carter
Design: Arthur Carter, AustenHouse

Library and Archives Canada Cataloguing in Publication Data

Soucoup, Dan 1949-
The Nova Scotia phrase book: sayings, expressions. and odd names of
Nova Scotia/Dan Soucoup

ISBN13 978-1-89442030-3

1. Canadianisms (English)—Nova Scotia. 2. Aphorisms and apothegms—
Nova Scotia. 3. Names, Geographical—Nova Scotia.

FC2304.S69 2007   971.6   C2007-901124-1

the fact some of these names are extremely unusual or mysterious in origins. Portapique, Folly Lake, Sober Island. Washabuck, Ecum Secum, Necum Teuch, Burntcoat Head, Baptist Brook, Conquerall Bank, Diligent River, Marshy Hope, and Mistake River all are curious sounding names and some of the stories behind these place names are truly marvelous. The reader will also find sprinkled throughout the collection old commercial brand names such as Reindeer Condensed Milk, Bottled sunshine, unshrinkables, Frenchy's, Pot of Gold, and Glen Breton. Civic slogans both historic and contemporary have been added such as Busy Amherst, Heart of the Valley, Gateway to Newfoundland and Labrador, Parrsboro shore, and Nova Scarcity. Old political slogans are interesting especially to those who can remember electioneering phrases like Honest it's John, It's time for a new start, Angus L is back, and the quiet man from Nova Scotia.

This captivating and at times humorous collection of words and phrases is not an attempt to define what has originated in the province but rather to cite the phrases that are important, essential expressions of the province and the people who live here. For example, wicked and awful as intensifiers are so often used today in Nova Scotia that I have included these terms although they are used constantly throughout the English-speaking world while more recent terms such as "whatever bro, homeboy, crib, sweet," still seem to be quite foreign in their Nova "Scotianess." However, that can and no doubt will change and future Nova Scotia collections of phrases at some later date will probably look more favourably on these strange new terms that are heard in Nova Scotia but are pieces of a new global culture, disseminated through electronic modes of communication.

One of my favourite expressions comes out of the old civic government's approach to public order. Most communities throughout North America have a dogcatcher but for many years in Nova Scotia, we had a hog reeve. As the public pig-catcher, this person was a county or municipality worker with the task of seizing stray pigs and assessing what property damage occurred while the animal was on the loose. Other personal favourites in this volume that I think somehow capture an essential quality of Nova Scotia include when she's payin', and marry too far. Two more are yaffle it and t'ick o' fog. But then again, this is a wicked list, something to crow about, a collection that you can go all foolish for, especially between hay and grass, if you're not born short and left over, a real corker, but then again, it won't cost an arm and a leg…

Acknowledgements

Much of this collection has been gathered over time from various written sources including the books and articles referenced in the bibliography by writers and oral historians as diverse as Thomas Chandler Haliburton in the 19th century, Helen Creighton and Clara Dennis in the early years of the 20th century. Others include Marion Robertson, Ernest Buckler, Thomas H. Raddall, and more recently, Lewis Poteet, Laurie Lacey, Mike Parker, and Clary Croft. As well, a number of scholars have contributed to our appreciation of the historic significance of intriguing place names including William B. Hamilton and Margaret Harry. However, many of these strange and exotic sayings have been collected simply by carefully listening to Nova Scotians as they go through their day-to-day lives.

A

A-A for Apples – During World War II, secret radio codes were broadcasted throughout Nova Scotia to alert citizens of enemy activities. Naval authorities used the code "A-A is for apples." According to Thomas Raddall in his book *Halifax Warden of the North*, a typical broadcast would begin with a "few bars of Rule Britannia and a mysterious voice calling 'Attention, all light-keepers in the East Coast area! Instructions A-A for Apples-will be carried out'."

Abeam – Widest cross section of a vessel.

Abide – Go along with it.

Able sailor – Descriptive phrase for a strong and capable person.

Aboiteau – Acadian device developed in the 17th century to create and maintain dykes by draining the tidal marshes around the Bay of Fundy.

About the best – "About" used as an intensifier emphasizing there's not much chance of it getting better.

Above board – Nautical expression for out in the open.

Acadia – Name for the early French colony l'Acadie that has been traced to the European explorer Giovanni da Verrazzano and the meaning "peaceful region." It is also possible that the name has Mi'kmaq origins from the term "cadie," meaning "a section of territory."

According to Dan Paul – Mi'kmaq writer and historian whose seminal 1993 book, *We Were Not the Savages*, went a long way towards a new understanding of Nova Scotia's history.

Ace in the hole – That one thing you can depend on.

Adrift – To wander aimlessly, without a rudder to steer a course.

Advocate – Harbour, village, and bay in Cumberland County. Origins of this place name are uncertain but Rodger David Brown in his book, *Historic Cumberland County South*, suggests the legal connection. He writes that in 1607, Samuel de Champlain gave the place its name le avocat, in honour of companion, French lawyer Marc Lescarbot.

Adzed her off – An adze is a hand-tool once used extensively for dressing rough lumber by squaring off one side. Adzing off a rough log floor would be to make the floor even.

After being there – Been there before.

Afterclap – Child born nine months after the husband has been away from the home. Afterthought is when a child is born many years after the first child comes into the world.

Afterdamp – Poisonous gases that remain in a coal mine after an explosion.

After doing – What are you after doing now, i.e. what are you doing?

Aftergrass – Second cut of hay. Also called rowen in southeastern Nova Scotia.

Africadia – Black Nova Scotia. The term originated or was first popularized by Nova Scotia writer George Elliott Clarke to note the historic black presence in Nova Scotia.

Africville – Historic Black community on the shores of Bedford Basin in north end Halifax. Residents were uprooted in the 1960s and their homes were demolished.

Aft – Nautical term for the back end of a vessel.

Agog – Sensational as in, "the news set the town agog." See also *Saladin*.

Agricola – The Agricola letters were published in 1818 in twenty-three installments in the *Acadian Recorder* and offered Nova Scotians keen advice on agriculture. John Young was the author but signed the letters Agricola. Agricola Street was later named to commemorate this popular series on successful 19th century farming practices.

Airin' to blow – Wind is picking up. Also she's breezin' up.

Air – Mistake as in "I made an air on that calculation."

Airy a one – None, not a one.

Alderbird – Common name for the Yellow Warbler since this bird builds nests in alders. The black and white Warbler is nicknamed Spiderbird due to a keen interest in hunting for spiders.

Alee – To go "alee" is to go to a quiet place, to the lee side of the vessel, furthest from the wind.

All bow and no midships – All front, no middle. This phrase aptly applied to the *Bluenose* since the vessel was smoothly tapered toward the stern.

All dolled up and nowhere to go – Over dressed, also, dressed to the nines.

Alleys – Playing marbles or alleys involves trying to toss and flick the glass balls into a hole in the ground. Crockies are big marbles.

All foolish for it – Really likes it.

All hands on deck – Everyone must turn out.

All hell broke loose – Major flare up occurred.

All my born days – Expression of surprise, "never seen the like in all my born days."

All our salt is wet – No more left, all used up. Fishing expression since salt was traditionally used to preserve fish caught at sea.

All out doors – A big amount as in "as loud as all out doors."

All your eggs in one basket – Counting on it, no alternative.

Always a day late and a dollar short – Too little, too late.

Always behind like a boar's nuts – One who is always late.

Always doctoring – Going to the doctor at the slightest sign of pain.

Amherst Shore – Community on the Northumberland Strait and the name of a nearby provincial park. Amherst Shore also refers to the coastline from Northport to Tidnish.

Angus L. is back – Political slogan for the return to Nova Scotia of popular Liberal Premier Angus L. Macdonald in 1945. Premier Macdonald had spent much of World War II working in Ottawa on the war effort and served again as Premier from 1945 until 1954. Macdonald's popularity as a leader was so strong that rival politicians nicknamed him "the pope."

Anne – Not Anne of Green Gables but Anne of Springhill, singer Anne Murray.

Antigonish Movement – The notion of community self-sufficiency through co-operatives was quite revolutionary in Nova Scotia during the 1920s. Two Cape Bretoners at the Extension Department of St.

Francis Xavier University in Antigonish, Jimmy Tompkins and Moses Coady, developed a program of evening classes for farmers and fishermen emphasizing skills development and self-reliance. The movement was successful and quickly spread to other parts of Canada. See also the man from Margaree.

Apast – Already has happened.

Apple Blossom Festival – Annapolis Valley's annual week-long spring festival featuring the beauty of the fruit orchards in full bloom.

Apple Tree Landing – Old name for Canning since apples were once the community's major crop and the fruit was exported from Habitant Creek.

Arcadia – Yarmouth County community originally known as Upper Chebogue and renamed after the vessel *Arcadia* was launched from this site in the early 1800s.

Ardoise – Community on Highway #1 between Mount Uniacke and Windsor. Name is French in origins and means slate cliffs, common throughout the area.

Arichat – Early French name for this shiretown of Richmond County was Arischat, derived from the Mi'kmaq Narichat or Anarachue.

Arm – Narrow section of water going in from the sea.

Arn – Heated clothes iron. Also, curling iron.

Arse over tea kettle – To fall down on your behind.

Article – Quite the piece of work. Not a very nice person.

As cheap as water and a slight more plentiful – West India rum in pre-Confederation Nova Scotia. Thomas Raddall mentions in his book *Halifax, Warden of the North*, that many Halifax merchants often kept a cask of "right Jamaica in mid-floor, complete with spigot and mug, for the refreshment of their customers."

As goes Monday goes the week – So the saying goes and on the other hand, work started on Friday, "will never get done."

Aspotogan – Peninsula along the south shore between St. Margarets Bay and Mahone Bay. Name comes from the Mi'kmaq Ukpudeskakum that can be roughly translated as blocking the passageway for the hunting of marine mammals.

As quick as a wink – Very fast. First coined by T.C. Haliburton in his popular collection of satirical essays called *The Clockmaker, The Sayings and Doings of Samuel Slick From Slickville*.

Ass backwards – Got it wrong side up, upside down.

Assburn – Aspirin for pain relief.

As scarce as hen's teeth – Very hard to get.

Atlantic Neptune – J.F.W. Des Barres' famous nautical charts of the Atlantic coast first published in 1783.

At least there's no black flies – Common saying about bad weather.

Auction gale – According to Lewis Poteet in his book, *The South Shore Phrase Book*, this expression characterizes the huge storms at the solstice (turn of the season) that are so strong that it is sometimes better to auction off your belongings and move than to stay and deal with the destructive consequences.

Automobile endurance contest – Early automobile driving contests sponsored by the *Halifax Herald* involving over five hundred miles of rough dirt roads throughout Nova Scotia.

Awful – Intensifier as in awful smart, strong, or good.

Ax – Acadia University.

B

Baccy – Chewing tobacco. Also, a plug or a fig of baccy.

Back a letter – Address a letter on the back for mailing. According to Marion Robertson in her book *The Chestnut Pipe*, prior to the introduction of envelopes, letters were folded and addresses were inscribed on the back.

Backbiting – To back bit is to bitterly complain after the fact.

Backburner – Spare burner on a stove. On the backburner means low priority.

Back from the dead – Person looks terrible.

Backload – What you can carry on your back.

Back lots – Back areas of timberlands common in early settlement grants.

Back shift – Night shift in a factory, mine, or mill. Also known as working the graveyard shift.

Backsliding – Old Baptist expression for sinning by returning to evil ways. Term became widely used to refer to reverting back to bad habits and nasty behavior.

Backstays – Lines in the sky from the sun extending downward. The lines suggest approaching rain (always from the prevailing westward winds) and are also known as "drawing water" or are sometimes referred to as "the sun drawing her stays."

Backwash – Undertow near the shore often caused by long, slow-breaking waves.

Baddeck – The name can be traced to the Mi'kmaq term Petek, meaning "to bend back" and according to historian W.F. Ganong, the word is descriptive since it is necessary to turn back in order to enter the harbour from the Bras d'Or lake. An early French map spelled the community La Badecque.

Baleine – Community north of Louisbourg originally settled as a French fishing port and named Baleine (French for whale) because of a whale-shaped rock situated at the entrance to the harbour.

Bamboozle – Tricked. The term comes from an old naval hoax (Spanish in origin) of thrusting up false flags to confused the enemy.

Banjo – A pan shovel used underground in a Cape Breton coal mine. The shovel was large and round like a banjo with a three-foot handle.

Bank a fire – You can count on it. Banking a fire means covering over a fire so you can use the hot coals later.

Bank dory – Dory used in the banks fishery that can be stacked one on top of the other. See also dory.

Banker – Fishing schooner that earned her keep on the offshore fishing banks.

Bank, hang, and switch – Late fall chores: bank the house, hang the storms (storm doors and windows) and switch to winter tires. Now you're ready for winter.

Baptist Brook – Stream in upper Lunenburg County that flows into another religious body of water, Baptist Lake.

Baptizing pool – Community swimming hole that doubled as the local baptism pool.

Barachois – French Acadian term for sandbar that is a popular place name throughout the Maritimes. Near Mira Bay in Cape Breton lies Maclean Barachois, a name that combines French and Scottish influences.

Barbels – Fishermen's aprons.

Bare poles – A sailing vessel without sails set while bare pole is a bare-naked man.

Barking up the wrong tree – Got it wrong. From *The Clockmaker* by T.C. Haliburton, Nova Scotia's first international author.

Barn raising – Old-time community based cooperative effort to erect buildings over a couple of days. The objective would be to frame, raise, and cover in a structure such as a barn as quickly as possible by having numerous men from the local community volunteer their labour. See also frolic.

Barra Head – Richmond County site. The name Barra (Celtic for hilly island) can be traced to Scotland's Outer Hebrides and the Clan MacNeil. The Barra MacNeils are a popular Cape Breton musical group.

Barrens – A semi-arctic tundra-like landscape that is common in certain parts of Nova Scotia including some Atlantic coastal sites and the Cape Breton Highlands.

Barrow them up – Old expression for the back-breaking chore of off-loading fish from vessels along the shore and transporting the catch by handbarrow up to the fish houses for processing.

Bar Town – Old name for North Sydney due to the fact that the harbour contained one of the largest sand bars in Cape Breton.

Batten down the hatches – Make a vessel or home secure from approaching bad weather. Also, button down the door. Batten your hatch means shut up.

Bay boy – Celebrated movie by Hollywood film director and Cape Breton native Daniel Petrie. The film premiered at the Savoy Theatre in Glace Bay in 1984 and went on to become a Cape Breton icon.

Beaten for your good – You deserved the punishment and will thank me later.

Beat out – Tired.

Beat the bush – Old Scottish expression meaning to go it alone – fight the battle by yourself.

Beat up – Sailing in the direction of the wind by tacking back and forth across the wind.

Becalmed – Nautical tern for a still, calm sea.

Bec' apple – Bakeapples that grow wild on bogs and resemble the taste of baked crabapples. Also Bakeapple Barren, a site in Cape Breton Highlands National Park.

Bed tick – Not an insect that inflects the bed but a mattress once made by "ticking." This process involved producing a closely-woven cloth that would be filled with various materials such as feathers, hay and even eelgrass, depending on the time of year, and what was available.

Bee's knees – Tiny issue, insignificant matter.

Beinn Bhreagh – Gaelic for mountain beautiful, the historic home near Baddeck of Alexander Graham Bell and his family.

Belabour – Hamming away at something endlessly, "belabouring the point."

Belly-flop – Failure, diving into the water stomach first instead of head first.

Ben dodie – Glutton, someone who over indulges in eating and drinking. Expression comes from the Cape Sable Island area. Other names for glutton include comglut and Tom Doty.

Bend over backwards – Going to extremes to help someone.

Ben Eoin – Cape Breton community on East Bay. Name is Gaelic for Jonathan's Mountain according to William Hamilton, author of the book, *Place Names of Atlantic Canada*.

Benny's Bad Lake – Naughty body of water in Halifax County above St. Margarets Bay.

Ben's Bread – Benjamin Moir started a small bake shop near the top of Bedford Basin in 1812 and Ben's Bread is still available today.

Berrying – Going berry picking. The best berry pickers are always able to "thumb" out the leaves and green berries.

Better a small fish than an empty dish – Better something than nothing.

Between hay and grass – The lean time of the year (March and early April) in Nova Scotia when the hay loft is empty but there's no grass in the pasture for cattle. In really bad years, the animals would show their ribs. See also make it to the grass.

Between the devil and the deep blue sea – In a wooden vessel, the "devil" is the longest seam in need of caulking and between it and the sea is not an attractive place to be. Also, between a rock and a hard place.

Between the jigs and the reels – Between the up and the downs, highs and the lows, it will work out.

Bible Hill – Community across the Salmon River from Truro. Name can be traced to Dr. Thomas McCulloch, a founder of the Nova Scotia Bible Society, who along with his son, Reverend William McCulloch, became well known for passing out free bibles.

Biddy – Hen.

Biffed – Threw it away.

Big Ass Lake – Body of water on the eastern shore near Moose River.

Big blow – Mouthy, without a lot of substance. Also, motor mouth, maw-mouth, and her mouth goes faster than her face.

Big Clams – Community of Grosses Coques near Church Point where one of the province's best loved restaurants (Chez Christophe) is located.

Big feeling – Full of yourself, pompous.

Big lease – Huge crown timber lease during the 1920s that saw the Oxford Paper Company out of Maine control around 500,000 acres of prime timber land in Cape Breton.

Big Pond – Cape Breton community on East Bay once known as Coal Cove.

Big strike – Steel workers strike of 1923 that escalated after the provincial police and the Royal Canadian Regiment arrived at the Sydney steel plant. Coal miners went out in sympathy and soon there was bloodshed and violence on the streets of industrial Cape Breton.

Big sweat on – Sweating hard, working up a full lather of sweat.

Big timber raft – The idea was a good one but it didn't work. Yet the attempts became legendary throughout Cumberland County. In 1885 at Two Rivers near Joggins, approximately three million feet of logs were strapped together with the aim of floating the timber to New York but the raft wouldn't leave the slip or even enter the water. A second big raft of logs did float but broke up at sea and finally, a third attempt was successful but the innovation was judged too risky. Much to the relief of ship owners, the whole experiment was discontinued by the lumber barons.

Billing and cooing – Kissing and cuddling. Phrase comes from the sounds of doves and pigeons.

Bill of Rights for Nova Scotia – *Halifax Herald's* 1937 campaign to establish a post-depression era system of social security and economic justice for the people of Nova Scotia. The newspaper campaign was accompanied by editorial cartoons produced by Robert Chambers.

Binge – Drinking spree.

Binnacle – Nautical term for the ship's box that contains the vessel's compass.

BIO – Bedford Institute of Oceanography. Canada's preeminent marine research station was first established on the shores of Bedford Basin in 1962.

Bird Day – In old Acadie, the Monday after Easter week was called Bird Day because Acadians would go to church to pray that birds would not descend on their harvest in mass and destroy the crops.

Birneys – Popular electric streetcars used in Halifax until 1949. They were painted yellow and so over-crowed during the war years that they were nicknamed "the banana fleet" by the military. But according to

Don Artz and Don Cunningham in their book, *The Halifax Street Railway*, to Haligonians, they were "old faithful birney."

Birthplace of New Scotland – The town of Pictou where in 1773, Scottish settlers aboard the ship *Hector*, arrived in Pictou Harbour. *Hector* passenger John Patterson did much to build and lay out the town, and is known as the Father of Pictou.

Bishop Pippin – Famous Nova Scotia apple originally known as Bellefleur and first developed by Bishop Charles Inglis at his Annapolis Valley home near Auburn.

Bite off more than you can chew – Took on too much.

Black balled – Dismissed from a group over an incident. Also, black-beaned out.

Blackfly season – Mid-May to July when going into the woods is risky at best.

Black ice – Dangerous ice that is hard to spot until it is too late to stop.

Black lung – Coal miner's disease caused from having coal dust imbedded in the lungs.

Black Maggie – Strange witch-like apparition that would appear around Catholic cemeteries in Cape Breton with apparent strong powers to curse and cure.

Black-polls – Nickname for the Laughing Gull because it emits a sound similar to "ha-ha-ha."

Black robin – Nickname for the Rusty Blackbird.

Black snow-bird – Common name for the dark-eyed Junco.

Black water – Mysterious sickness that afflicted horses in the old timber camps. Before dying, they would stiffen up with inflammation and their urine would become black.

Blagarding – Swearing and talking dirty. Old English term that is still popular in parts of Nova Scotia.

Blanc Mange – Traditional Acadian cornstarch pudding.

Blanket their sails – Stealing the wind at sea of another sail.

Blaze up a line – Mark out the boundaries of a timber stand for cutting.

Blind man's buff – Children's game involving blindfolding and spinning the victim.

Blind mush – Soup made with cabbage and other root vegetables. Phrase probably originated in Newfoundland.

Blind Pig – After Prohibition was enacted in Nova Scotia, illegal liquor dens appeared through the cites and towns and these "blind pigs" became the local hot spots for all sorts of illegal activity.

Bloaters – Smoked herring that has been cured in salt.

Blocked solid – So full nothing can move, for example, "the channel was blocked solid with ice."

Blockhouse – Lunenburg County community where there once stood a military blockhouse.

Blocking and stores – A small wharf and boat landing site tucked away in a sheltered cove and used by fishermen to repair gear and mend nets.

Blocks and takel – Block and tackle. Sometimes simply called the blocks.

Bloody Sunday – July 1st, 1923, when provincial police on horse back attacked striking steel workers at Whitney Pier near Sydney.

Blossombird – The Purple Finch is often called the blossombird due to its spring appearance around the time of the apple blossoms.

Blow'a gale o'wind – Wind is blowing hard. See also fair breeze o'wind.

Blowdown – Fall down of trees due to a wind storm. The fall down is also known in the forestry industry as a windthrow.

Blow-me-down – Cape Blomidon or Cape Blowme Down on the Minas Basin, where the steep headland and whirling tides draw strong winds.

Blueberry buckle – Delicious desert of stewed blueberries with dumplings. See also Grunts.

Blueberry Express – Nickname for the old train that traveled up the LaHave River from Bridgewater to Middelton in the Annapolis Valley. The train was so slow at times that frustrated passengers claimed they could jump off, pick blueberries, and get back on while the train was still moving.

Bluenosers – The first known written reference to the term "Bluenose" appeared in 1785 at Annapolis Royal. Loyalist Rev. Jacob Bailey writes "The Bluenoses, to use a vulgar applellation." The term was used to refer to pre-Loyalists Nova Scotians but it still remains unclear how the term originated although suggestions include the early blue variety of potatoes and the blue noses of cold Maritimers.

Blue Rocks – Lunenburg County fishing community first settled in the 1760s and famous for blue coloured rocks.

Blue sailors – Nickname for Chicory, an edible roadside weed that grows throughout Nova Scotia and stays in flower most of the summer.

Blue streak – Foul or strong language as in "barking a blue streak" or "cursing a blue breeze."

Boat people – In 1980, a large number of Indo-Chinese refugees arrived unannounced on the shores of Nova Scotia and were named the boat people.

Boat train – Train to Yarmouth that would take Nova Scotians across the Gulf of Maine by boat to the New England states.

Bobbin oil – Lubricating oil.

Bobble – Booboo. A newly constructed vessel that bobbles over on launching day doesn't float but tragically ends up on her side, unable to right herself.

Bobsleds – Two sleds joined together by a chain and used for hauling wood and freight over snow packed trails. The sled "bobbed" along the frozen surface.

Bob-tailed sheet – Nickname for the weekly wage sheet issued to coal miners in Cape Breton by the Dominion Coal Company. Bob-tailed referred to the company practice of cutting off the tail end of the sheet to show miners that no wages were due that week due to their purchases on credit at the company store. The company stores were called "pluck me stores" by the miners since the store usually managed to deduct most of their earnings.

Bochdans – Strange apparitions and ghostly forms. Term is Irish in origins.

Boddle – To buy votes at election. A boddler is a partisan political operator who attempts to buy votes at election time with bribes. See also chief dodger.

Bogan – Backwater. A remote channel, or still water behind or adjoining a river.

Bogey – Little stove on a sailing vessel.

Bog tea – Nickname for Labrador Tea, an evergreen shrubby plant with dark green leaves that produces a delicious spicy tea.

Boil up – Big meal over an open fire.

Bold water – Deep water close to shore.

Bone dry – State of Nova Scotia on February 1st, 1921 after a Prohibition plebiscite produced an alcohol-free majority vote.

Bone-knocker – According to Robie Tufts, the Yellow Rail is nicknamed "bone-knocker" by birders since it is famous for its weird sound that resembles dry bones being knocked together.

Bon Portage – Shelburne County island near Shag Harbour made famous by the novels of noted author Evelyn Richardson. Her novel *We Keep A Light*, was set on Bon Portage and won the Governor General's Award for Non-Fiction.

Boogieman – The Devil.

Booming – A boom is a chain of floating logs gathered together end-to-end. The boom contains logs that are floated together as a raft down river or across a lake on a drive. Booming on a lake in Nova Scotia often involved "headworks" that comprised a series of devices (cranks and ropes) that allowed a crew to winch a boom across a lake.

Booting her – Driving fast. Also gum booting it as in putting on gum boots (rubber boots) and heading out to work.

Bord – Common name for the working shaft or coal wall in an underground coal mine.

Born short and left over – Not able to take care of yourself.

Bo states – Boston states, short for the New England states.

Bottled sunshine – Old advertising slogan of the 1930s created to market cod liver oil.

Bottom has dropped out of the bucket – Disaster has struck, usually referring to financial misfortune. Also, the arse fell out of her.

Bow net – Primitive lobster trap made up of a large iron hoop and a trailing bag to trap the lobster.

Box from Boston – During the 1920s and 1930s, economic conditions in the region deteriorated to the point that many Martimers left to seek their fortune in New England, especially in the manufacturing towns and cities around Boston. A "box from Boston" was a special treat that included gifts and practical items sent by a family relative in the US to a dirt-poor, Nova Scotia home.

Brace – Two as in "a brace of rabbits."

Brandies – Submerged rocks hidden just below the surface of flowing water.

Bras d'Or Lake – Salt water lake system in Cape Breton. Name can be traced to a cartographical mistake that once placed Labrador south of the Gulf of St. Lawrence. Southern Labrador then became Bras d'Or.

Brash ice – River ice broken up into cakes and also known as clinkers.

Breach – To breach the water is to come out either partly or to jump full out.

Breaker – A wave that breaks out into white foam.

Break, mudding, and pickup – This odd phrase aptly characterized the chores involved in working at the coke ovens in the Sydney steel plant. Breaking involved crushing the coke into the ovens. Once through the ovens, the coke would be immersed into a wet mud mixture and finally, after the coke was quenched, it would be picked up.

Breechy – Ornery cow that goes breechy means going on a rampage.

Bridge freezes before road – Familiar sign in Nova Scotia warning motorists to be careful driving over bridges in winter.

Briggs – Old Scottish style pants that puff out above the knees.

Bright Light – Nickname for the old Victoria coal mine #4 at River Hebert in Cumberland County. In 1931, a gas explosion ripped through the mine killing five miners.

Brig – Two-masted vessel with square-rigged sails while a brigantine features a schooner aftermast and a barque has at least two square-rigged sails and one schooner aftermast.

Brin bag – Burlap sack.

Brindley Town – Old name for the community of Conway outside Digby where over two hundred Black loyalists settled in the 1780s. After Birchtown in Shelburne County, Brindley Town was once the largest Black settlement in Nova Scotia.

Brine in their veins – Sea in their blood. Born sailors, destined to spend their life at sea.

Broad daylight – In the middle of the day.

Brow – Log pile in the woods waiting for transportation to the mill. At break-up time, a brow of logs would be rolled into the river to start the annual log drive down the river to the sawmill.

Browse – Rub up against. What animals do – especially deer and moose, to certain kinds of trees. See also Moosewood.

Brudder – South shore term for brother.

Brushing – The hardest job in an underground coal mine that involved clearing out the heavy stone after it had been separated from the coal. Stone is much heavier than coal and a brusher's job was back-breaking work.

Buck fever – Rutting, buck deer in heat, also can mean someone is crazy.

Buckle down – Hard work. She buckled down and passed the exam.

Buck 65 – Not the price of a liter of gas but the mayor of Mt. Uniacke, Nova Scotia's very own hip hop artist, Rich Terfry.

Buck wood – Wood cut with a buck saw.

Buddy – Bud or Buddy in Nova Scotia can be literally anyone.

Bud the Spud – The chip wagon on Spring Garden Road in Halifax that serves just about the best hand-cut French fries.

Bugaboo – Precarious, a bit uncertain.

Buggers – Ornery characters.

Bully – Quarter bottle of ale.

Bummers Crossing – Old nickname for an area of Digby where Water Street intersects Birch Street. According to Mike Parker in his book,

Historic Digby, this section was a popular hangout for the "less fortunate seeking handouts from passersby."

Bump – Cave-in. Once coal has been removed underground, pressure builds up in the walls and ceilings from the overlying rock and eventually, slides and violent lurches can occur. An underground bump at the old No. 2 coal mine in Springhill trapped 174 miners in 1958. One hundred miners were rescued but in all, 74 men died underground and Springhill's coal mining industry came to an end after two major disasters in two years.

Bumper crop – Bumper crop is an abundant amount, more than normal.

Bunch – Less than a lot but more than a few.

Bundle – A lot as in "he spent a bundle of money."

Bundling bed – Steel wires were produced in great quantities at the Sydney steel plant and in the bar mill section of the plant, vast amounts were tied into reels and bundled together on the "bundling bed."

Bun in the oven – Pregnant. Cape Breton expression according to author Glen Gray in his hilarious book, *Da Mudder Tung*.

Bunkered – Loaded down.

Bunkhouse – Hastily built log house for lumberjacks.

Bunkum – Gibberish, nonsense.

Bun – Tear-off piece of homemade bread.

Bunting, bands, bunkum, and banter – Typical description of the gala activities on boat launching day in Nova Scotia. Bunting, (flags) bands, (music) bunkum, (nonsense) and banter (plenty of talk.)

Buried on the town – Old practice of burying a pauper in an unmarked grave in the town cemetery.

Burnside – Largest industrial park in Atlantic Canada located in north end Dartmouth and named after Scottish settler Duncan Wadell's tiny 19th century estate. Wadell's settlement was located next to a stream (burn in Scottish) and called Burnside.

Burntcoat Head – Site on the Minas shore so named according to author William Hamilton in *Place Names of Atlantic Canada*, because a settler was out burning brush one day and lost his coat in the fire.

Bushed – Marking out a winter trail by placing spruce trees upright in the snow to serve as a guide for travellers.

Bushwhacking – The old-time method of calculating stumpage without following a compass bearing but going on a dead reckoning without staying on a trail. See also stumpage.

Busy Amherst – Nickname for Amherst in the early 1900s when the bustling town's industrial output was second to none in Nova Scotia.

But still for all it's better – It's better all round.

Button down – Tighten up.

Buying a pig-in-a-poke – Purchasing sight unseen.

By and large – Happy state of affairs. Phrase comes from the sailing tradition where "by and large" meant sailing with the wind in a favourable position, towards the rear of the vessel.

By rights – What's fair, as in "by all rights, I should have gotten that job."

B'ys – Boys.

C

Cabbage – To cabbage someone is to get them to work for free

Cadiddles – Leftovers. Pieces of food that are cobbled together into a leftover meal.

Cabot Trail – Named after the famous explorer John Cabot, the highway across the Cape Breton Highlands was officially opened to motor traffic in 1932.

Calk boots – Steel spiked "corks" on lumber boots allowed loggers to dig into floating logs while working with their peavies untangling a log boom.

Callibogus – An old drink popular throughout the Maritimes composed of rum and spruce beer – with a pinch of molasses added for taste.

Calling for – Forecasting as in "the weatherman is calling for rain."

Calling on her – Courting, dating.

Call up – Phrase for "calling up" a moose or deer during hunting season. The hunter with the best knack for calling was able to attract a buck deer or moose during the fall mating season.

Calv'd – Cow just calv'd a newborn.

Came in on the fog – No one is sure how it got here so it must have came in "on the fog."

Camp Aldershot – World War II advanced infantry training center outside Kentville in the Annapolis Valley.

Camperdown – Site near Herring Cove at the mouth of Halifax Harbour where in 1798, the Duke of Kent first established his telegraph system of flags and signals. Camperdown became the site of the Marconi Wireless station prior to World War I, and hosted a large naval radio base during World War II.

Camp Norway – Location in Lunenburg County where during World War II, Norwegians trained for military duties and later took part in the Allied war effort.

Camp Thief – Nickname for the greedy and noisy Moose Bird or Gray Jay that was famous for stealing food around the old lumber camps. Also known as Whiskey Jack, Carrying Jay, and Gorby.

Canada-bird – Robie Tufts cites the White-Throated Sparrow as having a distinctive song that can be interpreted as sounding like "I love Canada-Canada-Canada."

Canada's ocean playground – Provincial license plate motto.

Canoe Birch – Old name for the White Birch due to its use in the construction of the birch bark canoe. Also called Paper Birch.

Can't find the potatoes for the lobster – Singer Bruce Guthro's recipe for fine chowder. Plus a bowl of fresh cream on the side to thicken as desired.

Cant hook – Wooden hand tool of wood with a steel hook used to pry and grip logs. Also known as a peavey, cant dog, pickaroon, and pike pole.

Can't see for looking – Eyes aren't what they use to be.

Can't work today, wind's the wrong way – Old time excuse in a black-smith shop for why the forge couldn't be fired up on nice hot summer days. Everyone took the day off.

Canvasser – Political operator at election time with the task of swaying fence-setters and getting these uncommitted voters out to the polls.

Cape Breton Giant – Scotsman Angus McAskill was the largest man to ever live in Cape Breton. He arrived on the island in 1829 as a three-year old. An average size child at birth, Giant McAskill grew to be a huge man and died at St. Ann's in 1863 at age 38. He stood 7 foot, 9 inches and weighted 425 pounds.

Cape Breton Pork Pies – Not a hint of pork is to be found in these little delicious desert tarts and according to Marie Nightingale in her book, *Out of Old Nova Scotia Kitchens*, "how they got their name remains a mystery."

Cape d'Or – Site at the entrance to Minas Basin where early European settlers found copper on the exposed cliffs.

Cape Islander – This unique boat was first developed by shipbuilder Ephram Atkinson on Cape Sable Island about 1900. As a gasoline-powered fishing craft, drawing little water yet highly stable, the Cape Island boat quickly became the Atlantic fisherman's favourite vessel. American name for cape islander is novie. See also novies and yanks.

Cape Porcupine – On the Strait of Canso near the Causeway is Cape Porcupine, named for the site's resemblance to the prickly mammal.

Caper – Cape Bretoner

Caplog – Pole used at a dock to reach over to an incoming vessel.

Careless talk cost lives. Don't gossip – World War II slogan seen on bill-boards and heard on the radio. Military authorities wanted Nova Scotians to be aware than enemy spies were among them.

Caribou – North Sydney to Newfoundland ferry that was torpedoed by the German submarine *Laughing Cow*, in the early hours of October 14, 1942. Of the 238 passengers aboard, only 101 survived.

Carried it to extremes – Went overboard with it.

Carrying on – Acting up or partying too much.

Car – Wooden lobster cage for storing live lobsters.

Carry-out – Take out food or liquor.

Casket – Begun in 1852 at Antigonish as a weekly newspaper, the *Casket* is still published today.

Cask – Wooden barrel or puncheon made of staves (thin pieces of wood that are placed edge to edge) and secured by hoops. The maker of the cask is a cooper.

Castle Frederick – Five hundred-acre farming site in Falmouth once owned by Acadian Pierre Landry and deeded to English military officer J.F.W. DesBarres in the 1760s. DesBarres developed the rich marshland into a substantial agricultural operation called Castle Frederick.

Catch over – Water that first freezes over such as, "it was so cold last night, the river caught-over."

Catchy – Nickname for the young flunkey or gofer on a salt bank schooner.

Catfish – Atlantic wolf fish now called monkfish.

Cat house – Whorehouse.

Cat's Eye – Semi-precious stone found around Minas Basin and the Parrsboro shore.

Cat tails – Bulrushes.

Caulking and hawsing – Making a wooden vessel watertight. Caulking on deck involved laying strips of oakum and cotton between the planking while hawsing involved a similar operation below deck.

Causeway – Canso Causeway connecting the mainland to Cape Breton across the Strait of Canso.

CBRM – Cape Breton Regional Municipality, the new (1995) regional municipality in industrial Cape Breton.

Ceilidh – Semi-informal gathering of musicians and friends that usually ends up as a Maritime kitchen party. The term may have originated overseas but is now well used throughout Atlantic Canada.

Cellar porch – Lunenburg County term for an outside entrance to a cellar.

Celtic Colours – Cape Breton's International music festival held each October throughout the island.

CFA's – Come from away. Person from anywhere other than Nova Scotia.

Chain runner – Cape Breton coal mining term for a worker with the job of hooking heavy rope to coal cars in order to haul the loads in and out of a section in the mines.

Chamber pot – Old pre-indoor plumbing pot that was used overnight to save having to go outdoors to the outhouse.

Chamber – Upstairs sleeping quarters in a house.

Chameau – Nova Scotia's most famous treasure ship went down in 1725 off Louisbourg. In 1966, *Le Chameau* was discovered by Cape Breton treasure seekers.

Chandler – Company that provides outfitting services to sea-going vessels.

Change your tack – Move in a new direction.

Charm the heart of a grindstone – Very charming. Also, charm the birds out of the trees.

Cheapside – Old Halifax public "green" market between Hollis Street and Bedford Row and now called Ondaatje Court. Named after London's Cheapside market.

Chebucto – Original name for Halifax Harbour derived from the Mi'kmaq Chebookt, meaning "great bay."

Chedabucto – Bay that connects the Atlantic Ocean with the Canso Strait. Name is derived from the Mi'kmaq Sedabooktook and means "bay that runs far back."

Cherry-bird – Cherries are a favourite fruit of the Cedar Waxwing and in areas where cherries are grown commercially, the bird is nicknamed "cherry-bird."

Chewing the fat – Talking about this and that. Shooting the breeze.

Chezzetcook – Harbour, village, river, and lake on the eastern shore. According to Mi'kmaq scholar Silas Rand, the name came from the Mi'kmaq Chesetkook and means "flowing rapidly in various directions."

Chicken cock church – Nickname for the Little Dutch Church in Halifax where a chicken weathervane sits at the top of the steeple.

Chickens take shelter before rain – Weather lore that also claims horses and cows act up before a storm.

Chief dodger – Political savvy agent known to do almost anything at election time to convince a non-committed voter to cast their ballot for the right party.

Chimley – Chimney.

Chimney Corner – Community near Margaree Harbour named for the shape of a local rock.

Chips – Tiny pieces of waste wood produced as a by-product in a sawmill operation. Also the common name for potato chips and French fries.

Chock-a-block – Crowed, full up and in need of nothing further. To a mariner, "chock-a-block" means lines are as tight as possible.

Choked up – Didn't complete the job.

Chowdered it up – Mixed up, got much too complicated and ended up getting screwed up.

Christmas stopper – That one special gift that seems to over shadow everything else under the Christmas tree.

Christmas tree – Bright shinning fishing lure.

Chubb – Sucker fish and considered worthless by fishermen. "I went trout fishing but caught nothing but chubb."

Chuck – Throw as in "that stove sure chucks out the heat." Also, a chuck is a two and a half square pillar of timber that holds up an underground roof in a coal mine.

Chumming – Chum-fishing involves mixing up a concoction of ground herring and flour and then throwing the feed over the side of a boat to attract fish. Chum bait could be made from a number of different fish "offal" or refuse. Gurry or curry was another fish waste byproduct, a sticky oil that could be used to grease skids and haul boats back and forth from the water.

Church built in a day – The Church of Our Lady of Sorrows that stands in the Catholic cemetery in south end Halifax and was indeed erected by two hundred parishioners over the course of one day.

Church Point – Next to Université Ste. Anne at Pointe de l'Église stands St. Mary's Church, the largest wooden church in North America.

Circle – Social group of women as in "her circle of friends."

Clammer – One who digs clams.

Clap your trap – Shut your mouth.

Clawing tree – Favourite tree for a bear to claw and rub up against. Also the browsing tree. See moosewood as well.

Clean sweep – Fresh start. Nautical expression for the effects of a big storm running over the deck of a vessel sweeping it clean.

Clink – Jail or prison.

Clipping along – Moving at a fast pace.

Clod hoppers – Big, heavy pair of boots.

Close to the bone – Tight, living on the edge and just scraping by.

Closing in – Getting dark, as in "the night is closing in."

Coal in their blood – Once a coal miner, always a coal miner. In 1958, a rescued miner from the Springhill Mining Disaster who had been trapped underground for several days, was asked if he would go back to mining. He said. "Coal is in my blood just like you can see it in the lines of my face. Sure I'll go back."

Coalin' up – Taking on coal, loading on coal into the hole of a ship or on to a coal-burning locomotive.

Coaltown – Nickname for about a dozen communities throughout northern Nova Scotia.

Coast Guard – Name of the Shelburne newspaper.

Cobequid – Mountain range and a bay within the Bay of Fundy. Mi'kmaq in origin (Wakobetgitk) meaning "end of the rushing waters."

Cock of the walk – Conceited. Also cocky.

Codding – South shore expression for teasing or kidding.

Cod-fish point – Baccaro near Cape Sable Island. Word derives from Baccolaos, the Basque word for cod fish.

Cold toast – Unappealing. Can also refer to a lost opportunity.

Collier – Vessel that transports coal to coaling stations.

Come aboard – To come onto a vessel or enter a dwelling usually with a purpose, perhaps to set something straight, undertake a fixing, etc.

Come a davy on it – To pull hard according to Lewis Poteet in his *South Shore Phrase Book*.

Come-by-chance – In Newfoundland, Come By Chance is a community at the head of Placentia Bay but in Cape Breton, come-by-chance means an illegitimate child.

Come hell or high water – It will get done regardless of the consequences.

Communion biscuits – Molasses cookies baked in large quantities by Presbyterians throughout Cape Breton during the old sacramental season.

Conch-shell road – Hard surface road made out of sea shells.

Concrete man – Local name for Charlie MacDonald, artist, socialist, and businessman who operated a concrete business in Kentville for many years until he gave away the business to his employees. Born in 1874, MacDonald died in 1967.

Condemn – Unfit, in need of major repair as in "the authorities condemned the house."

Congrés Mondial Acadien – The massive Acadian heritage festival that took place in Nova Scotia during the month of August, 2004.

Confess – To testify or come forward at a church or prayer meeting to admit passed sins.

Conquerall Bank – Site on the LaHave River (French for harbour) that can be traced back to a settler named George Fancy who supposedly cried "this conquers all" after arriving on the river.

Cookee – Cook's helper or assistant in a logging camp.

Cooking up a batch – Making moonshine or hooch.

Cooking with oil – Modern and fast. While much of North America switched from coal and wood to gas stoves after WW II, Nova Scotia did not but many homes converted to oil-cooking appliances. Thus the "cooking with oil" expression.

Coosie – South shore term for a make-shift toboggan that would be quickly constructed out of hardwood and animal hide, and used by hunters to transport moose or deer out of the woods.

Corduroyed it – A corduroy road consisted of logs placed side by side in order to plug the wet spots. The road then became passable for a horse and wagon.

Corker – A real corker is big news. Can be a severe storm, big party, or even a dosey of a bump on your head.

Cost an arm and a leg – Quite expensive.

Couldn't fight his way out of a brown paper bag – Not a very good scrapper.

Counting crows: Seven crows a secret never to be told – Writer Ernest Buckler grew up on South Mountain over looking the Annapolis Valley and recalled this childhood rhyme about crows in his memoir, *Ox Bells and Fireflies*. "One crow sorrow, two crows joy, three crows a wedding, four crows a boy, five crows silver, six crow gold and seven crows a secret never to be told."

Couple – Several, more than two.

Cow couchant – A group of cows lying out in a pasture.

Cow dung – Manure patties that harden up after being sun-baked in the pasture.

Cow's milk – Pure home milk direct from the cow, not store-bought.

Cow tongue – Wild edible plant officially called Clintonia but also known in Nova Scotia as cow tongue, snakeberry, and dogberry. It grows on the forest floor and tastes much like cucumber.

Cracker room – Section in a lobster cannery where lobsters are cracked open.

Crachie – Small mongrel dog.

Cracklin – Dish that included salt fish and salt pork scraps cooked until they made a cracking sound.

Crack on – Nautical phrase for adding on more sail in order to go faster.

Cramp your style – Screw you up, throw a monkey wrench into the mix. Origin of this phrase is nautical. Also, crimp your style.

Cram – To squeeze it in.

Crank – A crank is a complainer.

Craper – Shit house.

Crazy quilt – Patchwork quilt made with bright blocks sewn together. Other noted traditional Nova Scotian quilt designs were called hole-in-the-wall and wedding ring.

Creamed – Hit hard as in "the goalie got creamed on that last shot." Also, creamed it is to ace it as in, "I creamed the exam."

Crick – Creek.

Critter – Barnyard animals especially cows and steers but also a horse or sheep.

Crooked as a stove pipe – Bent, also crooked as a cork screw.

Cross, The – Common name for the intersection of many crossroads throughout rural Nova Scotia. From New Ross in Lunenburg County to St. Andrews in Antigonish County, The Cross is a well known local term for a crossroad.

Chow down – Sit down meal.

Cross pile – To pile logs or wood at right angles in order to create stability in the pile and help keep the lumber from getting damp.

Crow about it – Brag about something.

Cruddy – Food that has gone sour or left unattended.

Crusin' for a brusin' – Heading for a confrontation, towards a showdown if you keep it up.

Crusty – Cranky.

Crow's nest – A lookout.

Crying out loud – The phrase means "oh for pete's sake," or "for good heavens."

Cubby hole – Small closet or hole-in-the-wall.

Cull – Reduce the number. Cull can also mean to sort out or grade fish. Cull apples were inferior fruit made into apple juice or fed to livestock.

Cult – Nickname for any new religious or new-age group that has settled in Nova Scotia over the past few decades.

Cumberland Ram – Local name for the Amherst-born, Father of Confederation, Sir Charles Tupper. Tupper was described by Wilfred Laurier as both exceeding courageous and defiance.

Cure – To cure fish means processing as in cleaning, salting, and drying.

Curly Birch – Nickname for Yellow Birch, also called hard birch.

Cuss until the air is blue – A lot of swearing.

Cutch – Before the era of synthetic materials, fishermen used cotton nets and sails and to prevent rotting and algae growth, a catechuic tanning resin called "cutch" was used to dye the cotton.

Cutest church – The little Riverside Church at Bang Falls in Queens County. The United Baptist Church was built in the early 1900s and was once selected by newspaper journalists as Nova Scotia's smallest and cutest church.

Cuties Hollow – This waterfall is on the James River north of Marshy Hope but the origins of the name are unclear.

Cut, peeled, and piled – What you had to do to pulpwood before you could get paid.

Cut, shoot, and load – Coal mining phrase for the early method of mining coal underground. Cutting into the seam was done first and then miners would "shoot" powder into the cut holes in order to bring the coal down. Finally, the loose coal would be loaded on to coal cars and hauled up to the surface.

Cut, split and delivered – A typical advertisement for firewood. "I'll take two cords of hardwood please, no poplar, 14 inches in length, and I hope it was cut last winter so it's dry enough to burn."

Cutthroat – Descriptive term for a person who is ruthless. Also used in the fishing industry as a nickname for the cutter and splitter.

Cuttin' and fallin' – Working in the lumber woods, cutting trees and making sure they fall straight down and don't get hung up in other trees. A good chopper and a good faller could each log several thousand feet of lumber on a good day.

Cutting and stooking – Harvesting hay, wheat, and oats in days past involved mowing the crop and "stooking" it to dry, i.e., standing it up in bundles.

CVR – Cornwallis Valley Railway that once ran passenger and freight trains between Kentville and Kingsport.

D

Dabber – Bingo marker.

Daddy oakum – Hanging festoons of tree fiber that cling to old trees in sheltered parts of the forest.

Dagger Woods – Eerily thick woods in Antigonish County where many years ago, a murder was supposedly committed with a dagger.

Daks Day – Old Lunenburg County name for Groundhog Day. Dacks is the German term for badger, the animal in Germany that closely resembles the groundhog.

Dal – Dalhousie University.

Damn good thumpin' – Beating.

Damn Presbyterian flies – Cursing another person's religion. Expression was collected in Lunenburg County by writer Laurie lacey.

Dancing beggars – Shelburne area phrase for some old-time Loyalist settlers who arrived ill equipped to earn a living from farming or fishing but loved pageants and theatrical engagements.

Dandelion greens and fried gaspereau – This meal is the official start to spring according to Norman Creighton in his book, *Talk About the Maritimes*. Others might argue that a big feed of smelts and fiddleheads is more appetizing but then again, a jag of brook trout and fresh asparagus is hard to beat

Dander up – Temper flares up.

Dappick – Stupid, as in "don't be so dappick."

Dawdling – Wasting time.

Dead as a door nail – Lifeless, showing no signs of coming around. Also, deaf as a door nail.

Deadeye – Hardwood block with a hole in the middle to allow a rope to go through the wood. Used in masting and rigging of sailing vessels.

Deadman – Pole propped against a leaning tree to prevent it from falling down.

Dead off – Dead straight or in a straight direction as in, "dead off the point stands the island."

Dead reckon – Straight on. Also dead ringer meaning the exact or identical as in, "she's a dead ringer for Dolly Parton."

Dead soldier – Empty liquor bottle.

Dead to the world – Sound asleep.

Deadwood – A person who doesn't contribute.

Deal – Cut spruce, fir, or pine lumber once exported to Britain. Standard sizes for deals were three inches thick, nine inches wide, and twelve feet long.

Deal pad – Padding used by a lumberman to protect his shoulder while carrying lumber.

Decess and desist – Give it up.

Dedication Lake – In the 1970s, high school students in Musquodoboit Valley (place name is from the Mi'kmaq Mooskudoboogwek, meaning opening out) visited this lake and convinced authorities to name it Dedication to recognize their interest and commitment to the valley.

Deep Rover – One-person submarine built in Dartmouth in 1984 by Can-Dive Ltd.

DEVCO – Cape Breton Development Corporation established in the late 1960s to rehabilitate the island's economy after the threatened closure of the coal and steel industries.

Devil's darning needle – Dragon fly that could sew up a child's mouth, fingers or toes if they were noisy, naughty, or told lies.

Devil to pay – They'll be consequences.

Dickweeding around – Proceeding at a sluggish and disorganized pace. No clear explanation can be found for this derogatory phrase used to characterize slower than usual progress.

Didn't have a clue – Not very smart and didn't see it coming.

Die sly – South shore saying for dying suddenly.

Different slant on things – New point of view based on altered circumstances. Sailors used the term "slant" to describe the angle of the wind in relation to their sailing ship and each new slant produced a new position.

Digby chicken – Smoked salt herring.

Diligent River – Once known as Riviére Gascogne in the French Acadian era but after Loyalist settlers under a Lieutenant Taylor relocated to this area near Parrsboro, Governor John Parr visited the establishment and named the community Diligent in honour of the steady progress made by the settlers.

Dime a dozen – Very common.

Dinging – Putting a thrashing or beating on someone. Scottish in origin and quite common on the south shore.

Dingle – Telephone call.

Dingle, The – Dingle tower in Fleming Park on the Northwest Arm in Halifax was erected in 1908 to commemorate the 150th anniversary of the granting of representative government in Nova Scotia.

Dingwall – Stone wall on the campus of Cape Breton University nicknamed for David Dingwall. While a federal cabinet minister, Dingwall was successful in getting numerous federal grants and programs for Cape Breton. Dingwall is also the name of a Cape Breton community on Aspy Bay.

Dinner tub – Fishermen's wooden box used to store food at sea. Also the grub pail.

Dinner – Twelve noon meal.

Dirty – Bad as in dirty weather.

Dir wreck – Direct.

Ditty-box – Ditty-box or ditty-bag was made of wood and held a sailor's personal tools and keepsakes.

Divvy up – Divide up stuff.

Dock – Deduction as in "dock her pay for coming in late."

Doesn't know his ass from a hole in the ground – He doesn't know if he's coming or going, he's stupid.

Dog basket – Nautical term for the food tray that brought the captain's meals from the ship's kitchen.

Dog – Dogs were pointed iron grips that held a log in place on the sawmill carriage while the log was cut. A dogger would be in charge of "setting the dogs." Similar iron grips were used in the timber woods to grip and move trees around. Once a tree chopper had fallen a tree, he would drive the "dog" into the tree in order to move it.

Dog down – Secure it.

Dog house – If you are in the dog house you are in bad standing with someone.

Dog shelf – The floor.

Dogwatch – Late night watch on board a vessel.

Doing the trail – Driving the Cabot Trail, an annual pilgrimage for some Cape Bretoners.

Doldrums – In a slump or depression. Nautical term for lying in a calm stretch of water. See also becalmed.

Dole – Depression-era welfare introduced county by county to keep Nova Scotians from starving.

Doless – A do-less is a lazy, good-for-nothing so and so.

Dollar at day plus board – Pay at a saw mill prior to World War II. Lumber camps paid a dollar and twenty-five cents a day but storm days were payless.

Dollop – Rough unit of measure, a lump or spoonful of sugar, butter, etc.

Dolphins – Buoys set out to mark a passage way through a shallow section of water.

Domie – Close friend. Nautical expression derived from dory mates.

Donair – A gyro-like pita made with zesty meat and served with sweet sauce. This fast-food dish was pioneered in Nova Scotia in the late 1960s.

Donkey engine – Portable steam engine used to transfer freight onto a dock or logs onto a skid pile. In Cape Breton's coal mining industry, a donkey was a big drum affair driven by compressed air and containing a huge amount of coiled steel rope connected to a coal car. The donkey would haul these coal "trips" up into the coal face for loading. A miner who operated the brakes and air valves on the donkey was called a donkey runner.

Donkin – This community outside of Glace Bay was once called Dominion Number 6 to signify the coal mine operated by Dominion Coal Company. But to avoid confusion with the sister coal mining community of Dominion, Number 6 became Donkin.

Donny Brook – Stream in Pictou County near The Keppock named to commemorate the arrival of some rowdy Irish settlers.

Don't look a gift horse in the mouth – Accept a gift, don't be skeptical.

Dory – Small flat-bottomed boat that could be rowed and despite no keel, could also be sailed and outfitted with an engine.

DOSCO – Dominion Steel and Coal Company that ran the Cape Breton coal mines and the Sydney Steel plant until it was taken over by the giant British company Hawker Siddley. In 1967, Hawker Siddley announced their intention of leaving Cape Breton. See also Parade of Concern.

Double-bitter – Two-edged axe with one side razor sharp for cutting and the other side blunt for knocking down branches. A double-bitter Blenkhorn axe (produced in Canning by Blenkhorn & Sons) was for decades the axe of choice by lumberjacks throughout the Maritimes.

Double-cropping – Planting a row inside another row, for example, planting a row of vegetables between a row of apple trees in order to maximize land.

Double house – Two dwellings joined together on a single property occupied by an extended family such as a father and son or two brothers.

Douse – Deliver a blow or a knock out. Also, to douse out the fire. Doused up means finished up and washed up.

Down easters – Old American term for Nova Scotian sailors. Today, downeast refers to the Maritimes and some parts of northern New England. See also down north.

Down North – Cape Breton. In *Cape Breton's Magazine*, published by Ron Caplan, writer George Hermann explains the riddle of why north is down. "Before maps and compass directions were generally in use, directions were taken from the flow of current along a shore. 'Above' was where the current came from. 'Below,' where it went. 'Up' and 'down,' the same. In Red River people would speak, for example, of going 'up to Cheticamp' or 'down to the Lower End,' or that 'Cheticamp is above Pleasant Bay.' In these terms, Cape North is the down-most cape in Cape Breton." George Hermann goes on to say that since rivers on the Atlantic coast of North America flow from west to east, the Maritimes and New England have come to be known as "down east."

Down to brass tacks – Finally getting down to the real issue.

Down to the last shims – A shim is a wedge to right an uneven surface and down to the last shims means down to the last few details. Also, down to the fine strokes.

Dowser – Very important person in the old days of searching or "dowsing" for underground spring water. A dowser or water diviner would walk with a forked alder stick, witchhazel branch, or even a sour-apple twig until some unknown force would draw the stick down towards the ground where an underground spring would be uncovered.

Dozey – Starting to doz or nod-off. Sleepy.

Draegerman – Mine rescue worker with special training in using gas masks underground. German inventor A.B. Dräger invented the gas mask during World War I and Cape Breton miners were among the earliest pioneers of the mask underground.

Draggy – Not quite felling well.

Drailing – Fishing method where a drail, encompassing numerous lines and hooks, is towed behind a boat.

Drain on the purse – Big bill that is creating hardship.

Drank like a fish – Very big drinker. Coined by T.C. Haliburton.

DRA – The Dominion Atlantic Railway ran through the Annapolis Valley for many decades before being acquired by Canadian Pacific after World War II. The "Flying Bluenose" train was the pride of the line.

Each year in September, the railway ran an "Acadia Special" train carrying college students into Wolfville.

Drank the King's money – Old 18th century press-gang trick to strong arm a person into the King's navy. Recruiter would buy the person a glass of beer and slip a coin into the drink. When a navy officer arrives, he cries, "You've now drunk the King's money and you're our man."

Draw – Annual moose license lottery.

Drawn – To draw out or fulfill.

DREE – Department of Regional Economic Expansion. Forerunner to ACOA (Atlantic Canada Opportunities Agency) established by the federal Liberals under Pierre Trudeau.

Dressed lumber – Logs that have been cut and planed as opposed to rough lumber.

Dressing crew – Men at sea who prepare the fish for salting. Crew included a throater, header, splitter, and the idler. A fisherman in the handliner fishery got the name idler if he ran errors for the dressing crew all day and thus didn't have to endure night watch.

Dressing down – Reprimand, dragged over the coals. Nautical expression for the unpopular task of cleaning and preserving the rigging on a sailing vessel.

Drifting – Fishing, usually at night and especially around the Bay of Fundy with the boat and net drifting with the tide.

Drive-in – Now virtually gone in Nova Scotia and replace by the drive-through.

Drive shack – Cabin for crew undertaking a log drive.

Driving his pigs to market – Heavy snoring. Also, sleeping out loud.

Drokes – Little stumps of trees that are common on the barrens along much of Nova Scotia's Atlantic shoreline.

Drop a spoon, a stranger soon – Superstition from Shelburne County.

Drop – Drop us a line or "drop down" sometime.

Drop-seat – Popular invention by Charles Stanfield of Truro. His firm, Stanfields, pioneered the heavy rib underwear and drop-seat that allowed lumbermen and gold miners the luxury of going to the outhouse during cold winter nights without having to take the underwear off. See also Unshrinkables.

Dry as a bone – Thirsty.

Dry diet – Living on bread and meat with restricted moisture.

Dryfoot – Nova Scotia term (south shore) for one who doesn't go to sea. Non sailor or fisherman in a coastal community. See also hangshore.

Dryhand – Derogatory fishermen's phrase for someone who works without getting their hands wet. "He's a dryhand and only pushes paper."

Drywater – A site that was previously covered in water and is going dry due to siltation or a dam.

Dubbin – Oil and tallow mixture used to treat leather.

Dublin Shore – Unlike the Parrsboro shore that refers to a stretch of coastline around Parrsboro, Dublin Shore is an actual community on Highway #331 at the entrance to the LaHave River.

Ducks and drakes – Old skipping stone game that involves keeping a stone moving over the water while reciting rhymes beginning with "ducks and drakes." Phrase may have Newfoundland origins.

Duck in – Drop in quickly.

Ducking – Going duck hunting. Also going gunnin.'

Duck, The – One of three famous Halifax drinking establishments: the Liquor Dome, the Duck, and the Mid-Town. Also to dodge as in, "duck your face or you'll get hit."

Duds Clothing. Fancy duds would be splashy clothes.

Duff – In Newfoundland, duff is molasses pudding but in Nova Scotia, duff is coal dust. A miner who cleaned up the dry dusty coal leftovers was known as a duffer and used a duffing shovel. When the duff became wet and heavy, the duffer became known as a mucker.

Dumbdora – Pretty but not a very bright young girl. Bimbo.

Dummy walls – Walls built by coal miners in the "gob" section of a mine to try and prevent the total collapse of the mine shaft. See gob.

Dust up – Fight, argument.

Dutcher – Lunenburg County term for biscuit, probably from the German Deutsch.

Dutch – Norman "Dutch" Mason, Nova Scotia's own Prime Minister of the blues.

Dutchmen – The original Lunenburg County settlers from Germany were known as Dutchmen in Nova Scotia no doubt due the mispronounce of Deutschmen (men of Germany.)

Dutch Mess – Salt cod, potatoes, and pork scraps. Lunenburg County traditional recipe also known as house-bankin.'

Dutch Village philosopher – Titus Smith was Nova Scotia's first environmentalist and recorded many different kinds of provincial plants, animals, and bird species. He lived on a 50-acre farm in Dutch Village outside of Halifax.

Dwarf Cornel – Local name for Bunchberry, an edible plant growing throughout the province.

E

Ear full – Quite an ear full means being on the receiving end of a whole lot of talking.

Early bird gets the worm – Advice from the sayings and doings of Sam Slick by T.C. Haliburton.

Early to rise to cut salt marsh grass – Cutting marsh grass had to be done first thing in the morning since dew on the grass was necessary or else the scythe would quickly become dull.

Eastern shore – Atlantic coastline from Canso to the outskirts of Dartmouth.

East of ordinary – New (2006) branding slogan for Cape Breton.

Eat hash and like it – World War II patriotic motto since wasting food was considered a strain on the war effort. One housewife was quoted as saying that as long as her husband was overseas, her family would "eat hash and like it." Potluck was another meal that was considered doing your part for the Allies: "Potluck with Churchill today than humble pie under Hitler tomorrow." Other wartime sayings include victory is sweeter than sugar, guns instead of butter, and you need not hoard.

Eating – For personal use. Eating apples, eating fish, and meat, etc., would be small amounts set aside by farmers or fishermen for their own consumption.

Eat it whole, heart, and soul – Enjoy the food.

ECBC – Enterprise Cape Breton Corporation, a federal crown development agency established in 1987.

ECMA – East Coast Music Awards.

Ecum Secum – Community along the eastern shore. William Hamilton in his book, *Place Names of Atlantic Canada*, mentions that the origins of this name are unclear but may have come from the Mi'kmaq Ekamsagen.

Eel grass – Zostera marina grows along the rocky shores of Nova Scotia and was once collected, pressed, baled, and shipped to the US where it was manufactured into mats and quilts.

Electric City – Local name for a wilderness site in Digby County that was developed by the Stehelin family from France into a modern industrial center powered by electricity prior to 1900.

Elephant Grass – Nickname from south western Nova Scotia for a tall slender marsh grass once used to thatch roofs by the early Acadian pioneers.

Emptying out – Raining, the sky is emptying out.

Enough makeup to paint a barn door – The lady was lit up like a Christmas tree.

Eskasoni – Community on East Bay in Cape Breton. The name comes from the Mi'kmaq Eskasoognig meaning "green boughs."

European sucker – Valley name for a nasty pest that attacks apple trees. There are other interesting names for foul insects that attack fruit including the green bug, red mite, green apple worm, stinging bug, coddlin moth, and the bud moth.

Evangeline Trail – This marketing phrase originally included "The Land of Evangeline" and was developed by the tourism industry to promote the Yarmouth to Windsor route.

Every attention paid to ventilation and cleanliness – This 19th century advertising slogan promoted a private marine hospital in Halifax.

Every dog has his day – Wisdom from noted author T.C. Haliburton.

Everything went flat – Description of the Depression-era situation.

Expecting – Knocked up, pregnant.

F

Face cord – Less than a full cord of firewood or a "few logs short of a load." Also called a stove cord, a rack, or a "run" of wood. A cord of wood measures four feet by four feet by eight feet (128 cubic feet) while a face cord usually measures short in behind the load.

Face like a can of worms – Ugly. Also ugly as an axe handle, stump fence, or homely as a wire brush.

Facing and tailing – Old phrase for packing apples into barrels for market. Facing involved packing the first layer of apples stems down, according to Anne Hutten, in her book, *Valley Gold*, and tailing involved packing the top and final layer of apples in an attractive pattern with all stems clipped.

Fagged out – Tired.

Failed out – Closed up shop, went out of business.

Fair breeze o' wind – Stiff wind blowing.

Fair to middling – Ok to about halfway. Could be better but not complaining.

Fairy holes – Sacred Mi'kmaq site near Point Aconi in Cape Breton. Also called Glooscap's Caves.

Fall banking – Banking up the sides of the house each fall with straw, hay, eel grass, seaweed, or whatever else you can find to protect against winter storms.

Fallflies – Each autumn, bumble bees and other insects aimlessly drone and hum around since they are on their last days.

Fall gull – Due to its arrival in September or October, the Black-legged Kittiwake is named the fall gull by fishermen along the south shore.

Fallish – In the fall there is a change of season and this "fallish" feeling occurs because the cool weather has come. Also, the fall season.

False courage – Bravery that comes from drinking liquor.

Farewell to Nova Scotia – The province's most celebrated song.

Farmed out – Can mean site is no longer productive similar to a place being fished out but also can mean to farm something out to someone else, sublet, lend, etc.

Farmer's college – Nova Scotia Agricultural College at Truro.

Fart sack – World War II military slang for the bed.

Father's t'other end – Phrase for a new room built on to a house for a newlywed son or daughter.

Favour – To favour the wind or the tide means to go in the direction of the prevailing wind or with the tide.

Feast or famine – It's the extremes, either good or bad, nothing in the middle.

Feeder – Farm league or feeder system that grooms for the big league, pours into the big river, etc.

Feeding the gulls – Seasickness, as in wrenching over the side.

Feelers out – To put feelers out is to try and get a "feel" for the situation without making it too obvious and appearing anxious. Just sniffing the breeze to get a reading on the day. Also, to sound out is to make inquiries.

Fell off the wagon – Starting drinking again. On the wagon means staying away from alcohol.

Festival of the Tartan – Pictou County's annual Scottish festival.

Fetch a heave – Give a hand. Fetch up is to come along side as in "fetch up against that schooner."

Find a penny, pick it up, good luck will follow – Old south shore superstition.

Fine kettle of fish – Trouble a brewing, more than one bargained for.

Finest kind – Description of the best as in "finest kind of day" or can be the answer to the question: "how are you today? Finest kind."

Finger mitts – Glove-mitten combination that features a separate index finger developed for wartime use (trigger finger) and adapted to the fishing industry whereby a fishing hook could be baited without taking off the mitt.

Finnan Haddie – Smoked haddock. The phrase comes from Scotland and the port of Findhorn where the Scottish smoking process began.

Fire it up – Get it going.

First cousin once removed on your father's side – Definitely a relative.

First footed – South shore phrase for the first person through the door on New Year's Day. A dark-hair man was considered good luck while a light-hair man or a woman was thought to be a forerunner to a bad year.

First going off – First born child.

First good going – First available time when things are starting to go right.

First light – Dawn.

Fished – Hauled out as in "fished out of the water."

Fish fry – Big outdoor feed of seafood. Also called a lobster boil-up.

Fish Hawk – Osprey that mainly feeds on live fish that it captures by stunning dives into the water.

Fish ladder – The King Fish Ladder was first patented by Jim King of Shubenacadie in 1870 and allowed fish to swim upstream around dams and waterfalls.

Fish on the half-line – To fish as a hired hand with the promise of half of the boat's catch in exchange for labour. Owner supplies boat, gear, and bait. Also, "halve up the catch."

Fish or cut bait – Do one or the other, can't do both.

Fish or no fish – Either way it has to be done.

Fish out of water – Awkward situation.

Fish tale – A yarn that may or may not be true but don't bank on it.

Fit as a fiddle – In good health.

Fit-out – Get fitted-out is to get the clothes, supplies, and equipment for the trip.

Flag station – Less than a full-service railway station house. A flag station allowed passengers to wait for a train at a small waiting room or outside wooden platform but didn't offer a sit-down lounge, freight shed, or a ticket agent.

Flakes – Area on the edge of a fishing town where acres of wooden racks held split haves of codfish laid out to dry in the wind and sun.

Flap – Agitation, getting into a flap can mean a disagreement or simply creating a bit of excitement.

Flat calm – Dead calm on the water. Also, calming the waters means to quiet the situation down.

Fleeting – Coal mining term for fitting out the underground coal seam cutter known as the Dosco miner. A fleeter's job was to prepare the cutter for going into the coal seam.

Flies were wicked – Really thick and nasty batch of flies that bite hard.

Flogging a dead horse – Hopeless situation. Phrase comes from the nautical world where a dead horse referred to a sailor's debt for wages advanced while on shore. A sailor's reluctance to work during the dead horse period was renowned by a captain and became known as trying to flog a dead horse.

Floundering – Losing one's way from neglect or being worn out.

Flow gently sweet Afton – Robbie Burns' poem that was the inspiration for naming the Antigonish County community of Afton.

Flue – Inside chimney pipe.

Fly by night – Devious, not fully legitimate, doing something on the side without full authority. Phrase was use extensively in the taxi industry designating unlicensed cabs but has origins in the nautical world and referred to a large, easy-to-manage sail that could be set for night sailing.

Flycatcher bird – The Warbler, especially Wilson's Warbler that is known to largely feed on insects that are taken in the air.

Flying and crying – Shelburne County expression. When Loons are "flying and crying" rain is on the way according to Louis Poteet, author of the *South Shore Phrase Book*.

Flying axe-handles – Diarrhea.

Flying set – Banks fishery phrase for dory fishing where the main vessel towed the dories and drop them off one at a time as opposed to having the dories row out individually from the vessel to the fishing site. Later, in the flying set arrangement, the vessel would pick up the dories after the trawl lines had been recovered.

Fly in the ointment – There's a catch or problem.

Fly off the handle – Short fuse, gets mad easy.

Flypaper – Someone who insists on hanging around despite having outworn their welcome.

Foc's'le – Forecastle. The section below deck in the foremost part of the vessel.

Fogburner – A day when the sun burns off the moisture in the air.

Followed the sea – Went to sea, chose the seafaring life.

Folly Lake – Colchester site near Wentworth where Scottish settler James Flemming established a farm in 1762 against local advice since the land was quite rocky. In recognition of Flemming's error, the area became known as Folly.

Fool Hen – Spruce Grouse. So named fool or silly hen according to Robie Tufts in *Birds of Nova Scotia* because this partridge can be caught so easy and has little appeal to hunters. On the other hand, the Birch Partridge or Ruffled Grouse is difficult to catch and is considered by many upland bird hunters as the finest kind of game bird.

Foreign Protestants – German-speaking Protestant immigrants from Germany, Switzerland, and Montbeliard that settled in Lunenburg County and other parts of the Maritimes during the 1750s and the 1760s.

Forenoon – Morning.

Forerunner – A sign or sight that signals an upcoming significant event such as a death.

Forest primeval – "This is the forest primeval." Celebrated opening stanza of the epic poem *Evangeline, A Tale of Acadie.*

For medicinal purposes only – Excuse for drinking alcohol during periods when temperance societies were powerful influences in communities and drinking liquor was not allowed in public.

Forties, The – Community in Lunenburg County between East Dalhousie and New Ross. No one seems certain of the origins of this intriguing name although suggestions include forty grants were originally laid out and that the area once marked the point where the fortieth bridge was erected between Halifax and Annapolis Royal on the old Annapolis Road.

Fought tooth and nail – Fought damn hard for it.

Four sides of the wind – South wind brings rain, north wind the cold, east wind is snow, and west wind brings fine weather according to Laurie Lacey in his article, *Ethnicity and the German Descendants of Lunenburg County.*

Frank's Bandstand – Popular CBC TV music program of the 1960s. Frank Cameron hosted the program that featured local rock and roll acts.

Free-booters – Privateers were not quite ocean-going pirates but semi-official men of fortune.

Freeze the nuts off a brass monkey – Very cold weather. Also, shivering like a wet dog in a blanket.

French shore – Yarmouth to Digby in southwest Nova Scotia. A 40 km section of the shore in the Municipality of Clare between St. Bernard and Salmon River is known as the "Longest Main Street in the World" since the Acadian villages along this stretch of highway are continuous.

Frenchy's – Perhaps the most successful used-clothing chain in North America with headquarters in southwestern Nova Scotia.

Freshet – Small brook that overflows.

Fress – To eat like a wild animal or without manners. Bill Casselman, in his book, *Canadian Words*, cites this word as coming from Lunenburg County and the German word fressen, meaning "to devour."

Frigging – Exclaimer. A somewhat acceptable use of the F word.

Frolic – Community co-operative work event used for barn-raising, home-building, wood splitting, ploughing, planting, spinning, and other labour demanding chores. Neighbours would bring their horses or oxen, tools, as well as plenty of food and drink, and the day would be spent working while the evening would be a celebration of food, drink, and good cheer.

From little boats – Phrase commonly used in Yarmouth to describe how the area was first settled by Americans who crossed the Gulf of Maine in small boats.

From the frying pan into the fire – Got in to bigger trouble.

Frosh burn – Frosh bite.

Frost fish – Smelts that are caught in the winter through ice holes.

Frowned on it – Was against it.

Frying Pan Island – Tiny island off Ecum Secum on the eastern shore. Name is descriptive.

Fudge it – Make it up as you go along. Do it without a plan.

Full of piss and vinegar – Young and gung ho, not very experienced but willing.

Full tilt – Straight out, going full throttle.

Fully rigged and flags a'flying – Vessel is ready to sail.

Futtocks – Naturally curved spruce or pine used in the lower frame of wooden vessels.

G

Gabalashing – Lewis Poteet in his book, *The South Shore Phrase Book*, writes that gabalash means to lash a quilt with big, sloppy stitches. Galabashing is to run around in a party mood.

Gabarus – This community near Louisbourg has a number of possible explanations for the origins of its' name. Author William Hamilton writes in his book, *Place Name of Atlantic Canada* that it most likely came about as an Anglicization of the French name Cap Rouge. Historian William F. Ganong offers the notion that it may have come from the name Cabot's Cross and be one of the sites in Cape Breton where Cabot first landed many centuries ago.

Gad – A Y-shaped branch cut like a sling-shot and used to carry fish from the brook to the flying pan. Term may have originated in Cape Breton.

Gaft – Metal hook secured to a wooden handle and used to fetch.

Gall – Of all the gall! Cheeky and mischievous.

Galuses – Pre-World War I men's suspenders that were knitted in a unique ribbed stitch method.

Gam – Gossip. The gam was originally a social meeting at sea of two or more whaling vessels. "The time was when ships passing one another at sea backed their topsails and had a 'gam,' and on parting fired guns; but those good old days are gone." – Joshua Slocum.

Gamey and ripe – Wet and dirty clothes in a lumber camp.

Gander Month – April is the gander month according to farmers because the gander jealously watches over the goose while she is on the nest for the full 28-day hatching cycle. And according to writer Norman Creighton, April is also the month when the smelts run, robins appear, and of course the cormorants return to Nova Scotia.

Gang mill – Name for a sawmill with a "gang" of saws to cut up a log during a single pass-through. The log becomes a finish plank after just one gang cut.

Gansey – Nickname for wool sweaters favored by fishermen.

Gateway to Newfoundland and Labrador – Promotional slogan for North Sydney with its ferry terminal that connects Cape Breton to Port aux Basques. Prior to World War II when highways to northern Cape Breton were non-existence, North Sydney was also headquarters for the "Down North ferries" that ran along the coast to Ingonish and Chéticamp. Yarmouth once promoted itself as the "Gateway to Nova

Scotia" for Americans coming into the province by steamship and more recently, the port of Halifax is promoting itself as the "Gateway to North America."

Gaudy – Showy, too bright and shinny. Term is usually used to describe someone's fancy clothes.

Gave out – Passed away, died.

Gawk – To gawk at is to look hard at.

Gee – Go right in oxen talk, "haw" means go left and "whoa" is stop.

Get awake – Lunenburg County expression for wake up.

Get to rights – Get ready, prepare for it to happen.

Gig – Not a musical concert but a small 19th century one-horse, two-wheel, two seater, horse and carriage.

Gillans – Popular CBC radio program from the 1950s that featured a Maritime farm family engaged in real life farming situations. The series was developed and written by Hantsport writer Norman Creighton and continued by Ketch Harbour's Kay Hill.

Gill of rum – Old time measurement for a good stiff belt of liquor. A gill measured four fluid ounces.

Gimp – Stiffness, as in "not enough gimp to it." Also energy, for instances, no gimp can mean no get up and go.

Glitter – Icy cover of freezing rain as in, "we had a glitter last night."

Give and take – Compromise. A Thomas Chandler Haliburton phrase from *The Clockmaker*.

Gladders – Party person, always out on the town.

Glen Breton – North America's only single malt whiskey made in Glenville, Cape Breton, by the Glenora Distillery.

Glooscap – Legendary Mi'kmaq chief who's great deeds became mythic.

Glove compartment – Dash storage section in a car.

Gob – While at sea in a dory, a fisherman carried a "gob" club that was used to subdue a lively halibut that could reach a weight of one hundred pounds or more. Instead of hauling the fish up from the depths, fishermen often employed a hand-winch called a gurdy. The gob is also a well-known term in Cape Breton's coal mining industry. According to Rennie MacKenzie in his book, *That Bloody Cape Breton Coal,* the gob is a very dangerous place in a coal mine where the coal used to be. Once the section was mined out, "cutting the gob" would be left to a gob worker that involved the treacherous business of orchestrating a controlled cave-in by tearing out pillars and collapsing the roof. A gob worker's family could earned the nickname "the Gobs."

God fearing – Religious.

God's truth, so help me – Swearing on it.

Go easy – Watch words and semi-official policy of the Halifax Police force towards military personnel during World War II. The police were outmatched, out gunned, and the men on the beat turned a blind eye to military infractions especially regarding naval service men.

Go girlin' – Lumberjack talk for dating.

Going down the road – What many Nova Scotians have done for decades in order to make a living, going to New England, Toronto, and now Alberta.

Going through hoops – Difficult process to try and get there. Origins of this expression can be traced to the naval practice of having every sailor tightly roll up their hammock each morning so that it could properly fit through a standard size hoop.

Going to bingo – "As long as I can get out to bingo, I'm fine." As Jeannine L. McNeil notes in her article *What Comes Around, Goes Around: Bingo as a Cape Breton Subculture,* for a significant group of Nova Scotians, going to bingo is one of those simple pleasures that makes life liveable.

Golden Glow – Infamous hard cider originally called Apple Sauterne and produced in the Annapolis valley by Lewis Chipman. The alcoholic cider was originally produced in huge quantities – upwards of fifty thousand gallons were sold some years during the 1950s.

Golden robin – According to Robin Tufts, the striking plumage of the male Northern Oriole explains its nickname.

Go mudding – Mudbank sliding, a popular summer sport at low tide on the Minas Basin.

Gone to Tangier – After gold was struck on the eastern shore around Tangier in the 1850s, gold fever was everywhere and "gone to Tangier" signs were hung out in empty shops and offices throughout Nova Scotia.

Good as gold – Nice behaviour, especially for a child.

Good for what ails ya – Old promotional slogan for the marketing of health drinks and potions.

Go on with you – Don't be so foolish.

Goosetongue – Wild edible that grows in salt mashes and on tidal flats. The official name is Seaside Plantain. Goosefoot is a local name for Lamb's Quarters, a wild green that appears each summer.

Goreham's Rangers – Joseph Goreham's rough and ready militia that built forts around Bedford and Sackville and patrolled Bedford Basin when Halifax was first established in the 1750s.

Goshen – Guysborough County community named for the Goshen Society, formed for the purposes of organizing twice yearly trips to Halifax to secure supplies.

Got his back up – Got upset over something.

Go-to-meeting wear – Sunday best clothes.

Go tubing – Annual summer ritual of floating down the Gaspereau River near Wolfville in an inner tube.

Governor – An old steam engine device that regulates the flow of steam and thus the power output. Also, an affectionate nickname for someone with pretensions of authority.

Grading day gift – A present that children receive from their parents for grading.

Grand Dérangement – Tragic expulsion of the Acadians in 1755.

Grand Pré – Old Acadian settlement near Wolfville that translates from the French as "great meadow."

Grand – Yarmouth's Grand Hotel, originally opened in 1894.

Grassin' – Making out in the field or a grassy area.

Grass snipe – The Pectoral Sandpiper resembles the Snipe and prefers the marsh hayfields over the shoreline. Another sandpiper bird, the Spotted Sandpipe, is nicknamed "quiverwings" due to the rapid movement of its winds in flight. The Least Sandpiper is called "mud crack" because of its' habit of wandering along the edge of mud cracks on the tidal flats.

Graveyard of the Atlantic – Sable Island with its' 500-plus shipwrecks.

Gray-bird – Savannah Sparrow, a common visitor to Nova Scotia each summer.

Greased eel – Very slippery.

Greasy pole riot – One of the many military riots that broke out in Halifax. This one occurred in 1863 when the 16th Regiment were dissatisfied with the prizes awarded in a greasy pole competition. Soldiers fought among themselves and broke windows throughout the city.

Great Amherst Mystery – No doubt one the most interesting account of bizarre occurrences in Nova Scotia, not because of the unbelievable drama that played out in 1878 in downtown Amherst but rather because these paranormal occurrences by an apparent Amherst poltergeist were well documented by the townsfolk.

Great big – Quite large.

Green Christmas white Easter – Weather prediction from Lunenburg County collected by Helen Creighton.

Grilse – Young salmon.

Grindstone King – Amos Seaman (1788-1864) was a hard driving entrepreneur at Minudie in Cumberland County and made a small fortune shipping grindstones to the United States.

Gripe – Maintaining a "gripe" against someone is to be irritated with the person over an outstanding issue.

Grogging – Going drinking. Grog is a watered down rum drink that was first instituted by British Admiral Edward Vernon (Old Grogram) in order to save on daily rum rations since each sailor in the Royal Navy was entitled to one-half pint while at sea. To be "groggy" means to be unsteady.

Growler – A small iceberg that creates noise from grinding through the ice flows.

Grub – Food, groceries.

Grudging duty – Resentful about having to do a chore.

Grunts – Old-time fruit dumplings that first got its' name, according to Marie Nightingale, Nova Scotia's best known food editor, from the odd noises made by the fruit as it stewed in the pot.

Gulls or gannets – Old fishermen's belief that they will come back to life as either a gull or a gannet. Gulls are known to follow a school of herring at sea while gannets chase mackerel.

Gully – Deep hole in the ocean bottom near Sable Island that contains some of the most productive marine life in the Atlantic waters.

Gumption – Get up and go, as in "he has lots of gumption."

Gundy hole – Small hole within a coal mine used for ventilation and to pass equipment and timber back and forth between the coal seams.

Gunning tub – Floating tub use to sit in and hunt ducks.

Gurry kid – Gurry means fish guts and a gurry kid was a wooden box that held the stinky leftovers from "dressing down the catch" and was stored on the deck of a fishing vessel.

Gussied up – All dressed up.

Gut – Narrow channel leading out to sea such as Digby Gut.

H

Hackmatack – Fast-growing evergreen tree that is unique among native conifers in shedding its foliage each year. Known as Juniper or Larch outside the Maritimes.

Had the biscuit – Done in, finished.

Hags – The Greater Shearwater Gull was nicknamed hags or haglins by fishermen since large numbers would be attracted to fishing boats to fight over the offal (fish waste) that would be thrown over board.

Hailed – Signaled a passing vessel.

H'aint – Negative as in h'aint so.

Half a mind to do it – Will consider it.

Half baked – Not well thought out. An expression used to indicate something is not well planned out, and may be not complete-able.

Half cut – Just getting drunk, not quite loaded but getting close.

Half-mast high the signal floats – Nautical tradition that calls for the lowering of the vessel's flag to half-mast when someone dies at sea.

Half slewed – Drunk or well into his cups. Nautical origin to this expression comes from the unsteadiness of sails when the yards are not fully supported.

Half the town sells rum and the other half drinks it – Succinct description of Halifax in 1760 by civil politician Alex Grant.

Halfway River – Old name for Hantsport since it is situated half way between Windsor and Grand Pré. The river at Hantsport is still named Halfway.

Halifax currency – Shortly after Halifax was founded in 1749, local currency rates dubbed "Halifax currency" fixed the widespread Spanish dollar at five shillings while Boston currency paid six shillings per dollar. The notorious currency was finally taken out of circulation in 1871 when the decimal monetary system was introduced into Canada.

Haligonian – Citizen of Halifax. Dartmouthians are citizens of Dartmouth.

Handling – Fishing expression for transporting fish as opposed to catching it.

Handlining – Fishing without a net. Using line and hooks between buoys.

Hand pullers – When sailing schooners were refitted with engines in the 1930s, "hand puller" was the name given to a fishing vessel that refused to convert.

Hand wagon – Small hand-drawn cart used by fish or vegetable peddlers.

Handyman – All-round go-fer who is good at fixing many different things. Handy boy is a young go-fer on a fishing vessel.

Hanging-bird – Name for the Red-Eyed Vireo due to it's habit of building nests that hang from the branches of shade trees.

Hangshore – Too lazy to go to sea and is content to "hang" around on shore. Term probably originated in Newfoundland or the British Isles.

Hapjacks – Fried bread dough.

Hard cider – Cider with an alcoholic content. During prohibition, etherized apple cider was wide-spread throughout the province and contained apple cider laced with ether. See also Golden Glow.

Hard driving bucko served belaying-pin soup – At sea there were good captains, fair captains, and then captains from hell who would brutally drive the crew relentlessly while threatening to whip any idle sailors with a belaying pin, a short pipe of wood that fits into a series of holes, and serves a securing purpose.

Harden off – Before setting out small hotbed plants, farmers "harden off" these plants by gradually exposing them to the outdoors, allowing the vegetation to become acclimatized to new growing conditions.

Hard up – Not well provided for, lacking the bare essentials.

Hardwood choppings – Section in the woods where hardwood trees have been cut over and brush choppings are on the ground.

Hardwood hills a blazing – Autumn in Nova Scotia.

Hare's Lettuce – Wild edible weed that flowers each June and real name is Common Sow-Thistle.

Harks hard – Hard of hearing.

Harmony – Settlement near Truro that gained a reputation as a tranquil and friendly place and was named accordingly.

Harvest train – Trains that took Maritimers to the western wheat fields each harvest season. One such harvest train left Sydney in August of 1905 and before leaving Nova Scotia, the train was packed with over 600 men and women (women had one separate car.) The tradition of Nova Scotians assisting in the western wheat harvest began in the 1880s and did not end until after the Depression.

Haul a house – Move a house by literally picking it up and moving it over frozen land, ice, or by floating it.

Haul by the cord – An entrepreneurial teamster with his own set of horses would be hired to haul logs and be paid by the number of cords hauled out of the woods.

Hauled off and let him have it – Hit him, put the fist cuffs to him.

Hauled out for repairs – He's sick and taking some time off.

Hauled over the coals – Taken to task.

Hauling in – Along the south shore, this phrase describes a storm that is tracking east to south towards west while "backing" is a counterclockwise disturbance that is heading east to north (a real nor'easter.)

Haulin'time – Winter period when lumber crews would enter the woods to cut and haul timber. Usually January to break-up time in March or April.

Haul-over – Small canal constructed between two bodies of water to allow vessels to move freely through.

Haven't got a pot to piss in – Not well off and in need.

Having enough leeway – Freedom to do it right. Leeway for mariners is the sideways distance produced by wind pressure.

Hawker – Old name for a door-to-door salesman.

Hawk it – Seize it and pull it out. To hawk a salmon out is to pull it out of the river by net, spear, etc.

Hayseed – Innocence, wet behind the ears. Often used as a put down against country folk. Also, country bumpkin, and "did you just fall off a turnip wagon?"

Headers – Bank fishery term for boys or young men who cut fish heads on the deck of a fishing schooner. A header usually started out as a throater and then moved up.

Heart of the Valley – Advertising slogan for Middleton, due to it's location halfway down the valley.

Heavens to Betsy – Good grief!

Heave to and make a berth – Stop for the night.

Hector – Famous three-masted schooner that arrived in Pictou from Scotland in 1773 with Highland immigrants. A replica of the original vessel now calls Pictou home.

He drank like a fish – Big drinker. This phrase was coined by T.C. Haliburton's mythic creation, Sam Slick.

Heel of the hunt – Decision time.

He enlarged on things – Liked to tell stories.

Heenyus – No redeeming features.

He is skinny as a rail – Thin but tough because there's no flesh on him.

Hell bent – Determined to do it regardless of the consequences.

Hellish slow and wobbly – Apt expression describing the now defunct sluggish old Halifax and South Western Railway (HSW) that ran or perhaps limped along the south shore all the way to Yarmouth.

Hell of a lot – A whole lot, large amount of it.

Hello girls – Nickname for early telephone switchboard operators.

Hell Rackets – Site off Hechman's Island near Lunenburg that is named for the sound of the water.

Hen's nest – Left over strands of hay after a field has been mowed.

Here lyes the body – Opening inscription on most 18th century grave markers in Nova Scotia.

Hermit of Gully Lake – Famous recluse Willard MacDonald who jumped off a train during World War II in order to avoid military service and ended up living in a tiny log hut on Gully Lake in the Cobequid Mountains near Earltown. Willard MacDonald passed away recently, well over the age of eighty.

Herrin' and taters – The original comfort food: salt fish and potatoes.

Herring chokers – Fishermen and fishing communities.

He's a real tom-cat – Out all the time, running the roads.

He was boiling molasses – Making moonshine liquor.

Hew it off – Using a hand tool to plane and shape a piece of timber.

High and low piers – Throughout the 20th century, North Sydney was a major shipping port in Cape Breton and coal from nearby Sydney Mines was shipped from the port. "High and low" coal piers were constructed so that large, ocean-going freighters could load coal (high pier) as well as small schooners and coastal vessels (low pier.)

Highest tides in the world – Minas Basin area of Fundy bay where tides normally reach twelve metres and can measure seventeen metres certain times of the year.

Highland Game – Oldest continuing Scottish games that are held each year at Antigonish.

Highliner – The one who brings back the most fish. The champion fish killer.

High stepper walking on eggshells – Young woman in high heels.

High water mark – Line on the shore that marks the highest tides of the year. Debris and driftwood are left stranded.

Hilarious – Slang for delirium.

Hilled potatoes – Rows of potatoes hoed into hills.

Hilter skilter – Chaos, lack of order.

Hind side fore – Clothes that are put on "wrong side out."

Hit-and-miss – Name for the old hooked mats that were made out of rags. Each row would be from a different, brightly colour rag. This method was great for using up odds and ends of material.

Hit up – To hit someone up is to ask for a favour.

Hi-yi – Hello.

Hodge podge – Big mess of vegetables made up of new potatoes, carrots, peas and beans, butter and milk, (all essential) and whatever else you can add.

Hogging – Nautical term for an old wooden vessel that is starting to show her age. The bow and stern start to droop and the vessel sags in the water.

Hog reeve – Much like a dog catcher, a hog reeve was a county or municipality officer with the job of seizing stray pigs and assessing property damage that may have occurred while the animal was on the loose.

Holdfast ceremony – Old-time marriage custom whereby a rural couple without a resident clergyman could get married by publicly declaring themselves a couple and then have it officially sanctioned once a clergyman visited the community.

Hollow to the neck – Came to the table hungry and ready to eat!

Holy cow – Exclamation. Also, Holy mackerel!

Home side – On a log drive down a river, the home side was always the side of the river where the lumber camp was situated.

Honest it's John – Provincial Conservative Party's 1974 campaign slogan that featured leader John Buchanan. The Conservative campaign proved less than successful and the Liberals under Gerald Regan were returned to power.

Honey catches more flies than vinegar – Being pleasant gets you farther than being mean.

Honeysuckle bird – The Ruby-throated Hummingbird.

Hoodoo – Two-dollar bill that was considered unlucky by some superstitious Nova Scotia fishermen. Cutting a small corner in the bill was sufficient to break the bad luck of carrying the bill around in your wallet. See also queer one.

Hoodying – Lahave area phrase for skipping across floating ice cakes on the river.

Hoot and holler – Celebrate.

Hop beer – Homemade beer. Also, rotgut beer.

Hop in every drop – Promotional slogan used for fifty years by traveling medicine man, Doctor Herbert L. Rose of Port Maitland. Dr. Rose brewed his own secret medicine and traveled throughout the Maritimes by horse and wagon, hawking the concoction. According to Hattie Perry in her book, *Old Days Old Ways*, Dr. Rose claimed that if taken, his special formula would bankrupt the local undertaker due a to lack of business.

Hopping cars – Juvenile and very dangerous winter prank of grabbing on to the back bumper of a car at a stop sign and letting it haul you down an icy road.

Hop out and spare the horses – Old stagecoach yell to passengers when traveling along a difficult corduroy road. Passengers were encouraged to hop out and give the labouring horses a break. Some stagecoach lines offered passengers a discount if they agreed to get out and push.

Horizontal Churchill Falls – Description of the Fundy tides and their potential for hydro power during the 1970s. Fundy tidal power became all the rage during that decade after oil prices went through the roof and one tidal power station was developed at Annapolis Royal.

Horse mackerel – Fishermen's name for tuna, also known as albacore and sea lion.

Horse of another colour – That's another subject.

Horton Corner – First English-speaking name for Kentville.

Hot southern town – Halifax during the American Civil War when hundreds of Confederation agents and their blockade-running sympathizers pour into the city looking for supplies to further the southern cause.

Hovel – Dilapidated shed or worn-out shelter used to house animals in a logging camp.

Hove to – Nautical phrase for bringing a vessel into the wind and keeping it relatively stationary.

However she goes, what – Whatever happens happens, that's life. Also, how the cookie crumbles. That's the way it is.

How's she getting on – How are you doing?

HRM – Halifax Regional Municipality.

Hubbing – Tancook Island term for hand-grating cabbage for making sauerkraut.

Hummed and hawed – Indecisive, can't make up your mind.

Humphries – Durable woolen pants made by Humphrey Mills out of Moncton.

Hundred Thousand Welcomes – Clad Mile Failte. Welcome to Nova Scotia.

Hung in the middle and flapped on both sides – Gossiping tongue.

Huns – The Grey partridge is known as hun or a Hungarian partridge since it was introduced to Nova Scotia from eastern Europe in the 1920s.

Hupmobile – Car with an extra gas tank that would give a vehicle many extra miles on the road without having to stop for refueling. Used by both the police and outlaws during the dirty thirties.

Hurley – Old Irish ground hockey game that was transported to the frozen ponds of Nova Scotia in the early 1800s according to author Thomas Chandler Haliburton writing in the British magazine *Attache* in 1844.

This article establishes the basis for Nova Scotia's claim to be the legitimate birthplace of ice hockey.

Hurricane Juan – Biggest tropical storm to hit the center of Nova Scotia in many decades. A massive snowstorm nicknamed White Juan hit the province five months later.

Hurtin' unit – Not in the best of shape.

Hydrostone – North end Halifax concrete-block housing development that was erected after the 1917 Halifax Explosion.

I

Ice bird – A common bird in winter, the Dovekie is also known as the "bull-bird."

If maple sap runs faster, it's going to rain – Writer Gary Saunders' tried and true weather wisdom that is explained he claims, because falling air pressure causes the tree's sap pressure to rise. He also claims that fish leap before a storm (looking for low-flying insects) and that worms come up from the earth before heavy rain (or else they will drown.)

If the ash is out before the oak, you may expect a through soak – Old weather rhyme collected by meteorologist Rube Hornstein. The verse continues, "If the oak is out before the ash, you'll hardly get a single splash."

I'll be saying more than my prayers – Angry about it and will be letting everyone know.

I'll box you ears – Beat you up.

I'll tow that one alongside for a bit before I bring it aboard – Nautical derived expression collected by Lewis Poteet from the Barrington area and meaning the truth here is a bit doubtful and I'll think it over for a while.

I'magine – Yes, I agree.

I'm Alone – Famous rum runner out of Lunenburg named by its first owner due to the fact the Boston bootlegger had quit his gang to go into business by himself. In 1928, *I'm Alone* under Captain Thomas Randall was seized by gunfire outside US territorial waters in the Gulf of Mexico by an American Coast Guard cutter. The incident led to an international controversy.

Imperoyal – Site of the Imperial Oil refinery in Woodside on the Dartmouth side of Halifax Harbour. Name commemorates the Imperial Oil Company. Fifteen hundred men were employed in the construction of this refinery that opened in 1918.

I'm telling you straight – The plain truth.

In a family way – Pregnant.

Indian meat – Nickname for Cinnamon Fern, an edible plant that thrives in wetlands around Nova Scotia.

Indian summer – That pleasant and most agreeable time between the first fall frost and the next hard frost that signals winter is around the corner.

Indian tobacco – Bearberry was also known as Kinnikinick and the dried leaves of this evergreen plant was traditionally used as a tobacco substitute by the Mi'kmaq.

Industrial Estates – Controversial provincial development agency established in 1959 to help establish and promote industrial development in Nova Scotia.

In good shape – Things are fine.

In his black book – The British Admiralty kept a black book of rules, infractions, and punishments, and to be in the black book meant to be in trouble.

In his cups – Loaded from drinking alcohol.

In kind – Payment via a contra scheme that avoids cash, i.e. pay your wood-heating bill with fresh fish.

Intervale – Early 19th century name for Antigonish. In the book, *Historic Antigonish*, authors Laurie C.C. Stanley-Blackwell and R.A. Maclean note that the word Antigonish comes from the Mi'kmaq and was once taken to mean "where branches are torn off by bears trying to gather beechnuts." However, the more common interpretation is forked river since three rivers flow through the community into the Northumberland Strait.

In the fair land of Nova Scotia – Opening stanza in Captain Joshua Slocum's masterpiece, *Sailing Alone Around the World.*

In the offing – Close at hand. Nautical phrase for sailing in safe quarters.

In the pit – Working underground in a coal mine.

Iron steam kettles – Derogatory description of Samuel Cunard's pioneering steam ships that crossed the Atlantic beginning in the 1840s. Cunard proved his nay-sayers wrong and the steam-ship became one of the most successful 19th century modes of transportation.

Isle Haute – Island in the Bay of Fundy off Advocate Harbour with high cliffs that gave rise to the French name "high island."

I spoke him – Nautical phrase meaning I spoke to him in another vessel while at sea.

It's a wise nation that preserves its record – The core phrase of Joe Howe's famous "wise nation" speech that was given in Massachusetts in 1871.

It's time for a new start – Provincial Liberal's 1988 election slogan under leader Vince MacLean. John Buchanan's Conservatives produced their own slogan promoting their leader's experience "Strong leadership for new ideas." The Conservatives won with a small majority.

It will never be seen on a trotting horse – Don't worry, it's not going to happen.

I've got it forgot – Already forgot about it.

I wasn't born yesterday – Not fooled, wise to the situation.

I wouldn't go for to say – I wouldn't say that.

J

Jacket potatoes – Potatoes served with the skins on.

Jack of all trades and master of none – Someone who dabbles in a lot of things. This phrase first appeared in print in *The Clockmaker* by T.C. Haliburton.

Jack-snipe – Common Snipe.

Jag – Vague measure for a load but also having a jag-on means getting loaded or drunk.

Jakey – West Indie lemon flavored liquor that was shipped into Nova Scotia during Prohibition to serve as a liquor substitute. Also called tutti frutti.

Jaw-bone Corner – Site at Cornwallis where charismatic preacher Henry Alline established his first New-Light Church in the 1780s.

Jerome the Mystery Man – The strange case of a legless man found on the shores of Digby Neck in 1863. The Fundy enigma refused to explain his appearance and lived in the area for forty-eight years, known only as Jerome.

Jezebel – Female of questionable character.

Jigger – Small boat that went fishing with lure hooks.

Joggins – Community on Chignecto Bay well known for its fossils. Name is derived from the Mi'kmaq Chegoggin, meaning "fish weir site."

Johnny cake – Cornmeal and molasses served hot.

Johnny jump-up – Pansy flower.

Joner – Sailors believed that some people brought bad luck to a vessel. Such a person was called a joner, jonah, or a decess.

Jumped the fence – Gone over, accepted another religion as in the girl who changed her faith to get her man.

Jumping Jehosaphat – Exclamation.

Jury's out on it – No decision yet.

Just hanging – Ripe berries at berry-picking time.

Just plain guff – Nonsense.

K

Kaybreaks – Nickname for young loons.

Kedgeemakoogee – Keji, Kejimkujik National Park.

Kedgeree – Traditional Nova Scotia fare that originated in India as Khicharhi and was transported to the province by 19th century sea captains. Essentially a boil up of fish, eggs, rice, butter, and milk.

Keeled over – Fell down. This phrase comes from the nautical world where a ship would overturn. Keeping an even keel means proceeding at a normal pace with no worries.

Keeper of the Cliffs – This title has been officially bestowed on Don Reid by the NS Department of Natural Resources for his work at promoting and preserving fossils in the Joggins area of Cumberland County.

Keep the flies off – Very important spring-through-summer topic. Whatever could be invented or dreamed up to keep the flies off. However, fly dope had to include lard so it would stick to the skin.

Keep to the right – Campaign instituted in the province to alert drivers that as of April 1, 1923, cars were to drive on the right side of the highway. Cars and drivers adjusted well to the changeover but horses couldn't make the switch.

Keg – Small barrel of liquor that could be reused to store nails, flour, or sugar.

Keith's – The province's most popular alcoholic beverage. As they say in advertising campaigns in Ontario, Alexander Keith's Pale Ale is reluctantly exported from Nova Scotia.

Kerf – The actual cut in the wood created by the saw.

Kettle holes – Abandoned gypsum quarries that have created sink holes as deep as thirty or forty feet. Hants County contains the most amount of gypsum in Nova Scotia but commercial quantities are also prevalent in Victoria County.

Kiack – Gaspereau caught in nets going up steam to spawn. In some parts of Nova Scotia, kiacks can also refer to smelts.

Killock – Heavy stone anchor fitted inside a wooden frame. Also called killet and killick.

Killyfish – Minnows.

Killy Willy – South shore nickname for the Willet, the white-winded shorebird that when it senses danger, gives off the sound: "pill-will-willet." Also known as paddy-widdy.

King load – Teamster who hauled the largest load of lumber in a logging camp would earn the title "king load."

Kipawo – Most popular ferry that worked the Minas Basin between Wolfville, Kingsport, and Parrsboro. The name was an attempt to link the three communities. The 50-ton "Kip" (called 'dear old Kipawo' by Esther Clark Wright in her book, *Blomidon Rose*) now rests high and dry on the Parrsboro waterfront where she is part of the Ship's Company Theatre.

Kirkin – Old wooden tub one quarter the size of a barrel. A kirkin could hold anything from salted cucumbers to hand-made soap.

Kitchen meeting – Informal but sometimes highly productive get-together in someone's kitchen or back porch that would often produce an agreement or break-though deal when more formal meetings failed to generate results.

Klumpers – Big awkward shoes.

Knee knocked – Legs that walk bent inward, knocking together.

Knockabouts – Old worn shoes or discarded pants that lie around the house and can be used for casual attire or dirty work.

Knock him down street – Nickname for Brunswick Street (also known as Barrack Street) in pre-Confederation Halifax when the rough and tumble street was full of brothels and dancing houses.

Knock off – Quit as in, "he knocked off work at five." Also, a knock-off is a poor imitation of the real thing.

Know the ropes – Nautical expression that was coined to describe old sailors that knew the rigging on a sailing ship.

Krutty – Small and cheap.

Kuduffle soup – Lunenburg County traditional potato soup or chowder. Includes flour and potatoes with pork scraps, and once included sauerkraut but more recently it is served with the kraut on the side. Also know as Kartoffelsuppe from the German word for potato, die kartoffel.

L

Labouring oar – The partner who does the heavy work.

Laid up at planting time – Terrible situation for a farmer who must get his crops in.

Laid well – Nautical expression for a boat that behaved well while at anchor.

Lambast – Chew out.

Landing – The Landing on Antigonish Harbour once served as the town's waterfront. According to authors Laurie C.C. Stanley-Blackwell and R.A. Maclean in their book *Historic Antigonish*, the Landing also served the community as a popular picnic grounds.

Land sharks – Shipwreck hunters who pick clean cargo from wrecks. Also salvors.

Larrigans – Heavy waterproof leather moccasins or boots that were usually ankle length but could go as high up as the knee. Bottles of liquor could be secretly stashed in the tops of larrigans and smuggled with ease, giving rise to the term "bootleg." For a number of years, larrigans were produced in Bridgewater by the Mackenzie Crowe Manufacturing Company.

Lassybread – Bread with molasses (lassy.)

Last going off – Last time around, final round. Also, youngest child.

Last of the salt bank schooners – *Theresa E. Conners*, built in Lunenburg in 1938 and now the flagship of the Fisheries Museum of the Atlantic at Lunenburg.

Laughing'sterics – Very funny, hilarious.

Laugh on the other side of his face – Tables were turned and people are now laughing at him.

Launching day – Celebration day when a newly constructed vessel is released down the "ways" to slide into the sea. "Out chisel, down dagger" was often the cry that signaled the shipbuilder to release the dagger timber allowing the vessel to begin her journey down into the water. See also, wedge up, knock down dogs.

Lay in the potatoes – Plant the potatoes by laying them into rows.

Lay of the land – To get an initial impression. Nautical expression for mariners seeking landfall.

Lay over – Nautical phrase for staying over in port for a period of time due to bad weather or mechanical failure.

LCs – Liquor commission stores.

Leading line – Line attached from a wharf to one or more boats. Leading light means a prominent person.

Leading wind – A fair wind that will lead a vessel to its' destination.

Leak – To take a leak is to urinate.

Leery – Doubtful.

Les suetes – Local name for a sudden wind that rises around Cheticamp along the western shores of Cape Breton. Warm air off the Bay of St. Lawrence mixes with colder breezes from the highlands producing strong wind currents.

Let fly – Got angry and gave it good.

Letter bill – Bill received by mail.

Letter in black – Old-fashion bad news stationery that was designed to alert the reader to the fact that the letter contained some bad news. The envelope had black corners and the page itself had black around the margins.

Let the cat out of the bag – Secret no more.

Let the pot go dark – Burn the pot, let it go dry.

Licked – Gave up while a licking is a beating.

Lift – Drive, as in, "can you give me a lift home?"

Light must not fail – Light keeper's undying motto.

Like a bantam rooster – Small but tough.

Like the dickens – All get-out, fast, as in "ran like the dickens."

Like trying to climb Mount Everest – Hopeless task, about as possible as a snowball lasting in hell.

Lily-livered – Weak, lacking in gumption.

Limbo Cove – Old name for Pleasant Bay in the Cape Breton Highlands, once inaccessible except by boat.

Lion and Bright – Two most popular oxen names in Nova Scotia. These names were used for a pair of oxen. Sloop was the most popular name for a single ox.

Little bugger – Derogatory description, usually of a child that has a habit of misbehaving.

Little tender – Getting worn out.

Little X – In 1952, St. Francis Xavier Junior College opened on George Street in Sydney and served as the Cape Breton section of St. Francis Xavier Extension Department. The junior college quickly became known as "little X" while St. Francis Xavier University in Antigonish was dubbed "big X." Little X eventually became the University of Cape Breton.

Live and let live – Wise wisdom from Sam Slick of Slickville.

Liverpool Packet – Nova Scotia's most famous privateer schooner. The vessel had been a slaver called the *Black Joke* but had been seized by the British navy in 1811 and auctioned off to Enos Collins at Halifax. Collins and his Liverpool partners renamed the vessel and the *Liverpool Packet* became the most successful privateer to sail out of Nova Scotia.

Living gale – Real big storm, also called a wicked gale.

Lizzie dies tonight – Famous south shore ballad that grew out of a young girl's diary found aboard the shipwreck *Hungarian* in 1860. The girl name Lizzie did not survive the tragedy and her last entry reads: "The ship has struck and we shall all be lost. Lizzie dies tonight."

Loader – A miner that loaded coal underground. But it wasn't just any amount of coal. A loader would be expected to load eighteen back-breaking tons of coal during one, eight hour shift, an incredible amount of coal that had to be lifted entirely by hand.

Lobster smack – Nickname for a small fishing vessel with sails and a tiny deck or half-deck.

Lock Broom – Pictou County site named in honour of Lock Broom in Scotland by ship *Hector* settler Alexander Cameron.

Logways – Cribwork over which logs are rolled into a sawmill.

Loller – Good-for-nothing, useless. Also, lummock.

Lollygagging – Partying and fooling around.

Long Johns – Old-fashioned soft molasses cookies. This name arose prior to the introduction of cookie cutters when rolled-out dough would be sometimes cut in long strips with a knife.

Longshoreman – Fishery worker on land. The term now has been expanded to mean most marine dock workers.

Longside – Adjacent.

Looking at Westminster through the wrong end of a telescope – Charles Dickens' impression of the Nova Scotia Legislative Assembly when visiting Halifax in 1842. Province House reminded him of a smaller version of the English Parliament.

Lookoff – Well known site on North Mountain near Blomidon with a splendid view of the Annapolis Valley.

Looks like a child hurt on a cold day – Sorry looking sight.

Looks like he's been through the war – He's not looking very good.

Loose ends – Old mariner expression for frayed ends of rope and gear that needed to be tightened up. Not top priority and can be tackled when time allows.

Lord it over – Uppity, someone who tries to pull rank and "lord" over everyone else.

Lord's Barn – Early 19th century church constructed at Bridgewater as a Union Church meaning more than one denomination shared the church. According to authors, Sheila Chambers, Joan Dawson, and Edith Wolter in their book, *Historic LaHave River Valley*, the church was so hastily constructed that farm animals would often walk through the building thus earning the nickname "Lord's Barn."

Loud Lake – Descriptive name for a body of water south of Bear River.

Lowance – Rationing out portions of food, fuel, etc.

Lukewarm Tory – Somewhat a Conservative but not fully committed to the Tories as opposed to a diehard Grit who would support the Liberals whatever program they came up with.

Lump of spruce – Poor excuse for a ship. Also, a lump of coal would be miserable payment for a service rendered.

Lunenburg bump – Distinctive Lunenburg architectural feature whereby an upstairs dormer was extended down and out to create an eye-catching overhang above the doorway.

M

Mabou – Community in Inverness County well known for its musical and Gaelic heritage. Place name is derived from the Mi'kmaq term Malabo.

Maccan – Village in Cumberland County on the Maccan River. The word Maccan has been derived from the Mi'kmaq Makaan, meaning "fishing place."

Mackerel gulls – Three terns, Common, Arctic, and Roseate, are known as mackerel gulls in Nova Scotia due to their arrival around the time of the May mackerel run each year.

Mackerel sky, never dry – Streaky gray sky usually means rain in the next 24-hours.

MacPass – Halifax Dartmouth Bridge Commission electronic pass system.

MacPuffin dollar – Begun in the 1970s as a tourist promotion, the MacPuffin is legal tender in Cape Breton for the year they are issued. Puffins are fascinating little birds that live on the Bird Islands off St. Anns Bay.

Mac Talla – Gaelic newspaper (*The Echo*) first published in Sydney in 1892.

Maggot – Nickname for someone always on the bum. See also stemmer.

Maid of the Mist – Famous 19th century passenger ferry that once sailed Fundy Bay between Saint John, Digby, and Windsor.

Main-à-Dieu – According to William Hamilton in his book, *Place Names of Atlantic Canada*, this Cape Breton community near Louisbourg was first named Main-à-Dieu (hand of God) by surveyor J.F.W. Des Barres in 1786. Residents are known as Main-à-Dieuers.

Make a dog laugh – Real funny.

Make and break – Celebrated old one-cylinder (one lunger) marine engine that transferred the fishing industry from a wind powered trade to an enterprise fueled by gasoline.

Make away with – To do away with or get rid of.

Make dinner – Make as in prepare dinner. Also, make the fire out as in "put the fire out" and it makes wet as in "it is raining."

Make it to the grass – Late winter farm saying. Barn animals are looking weak from lack of hay but hopefully, they can make it until the new grass appears in May.

Make strange – Young child who acts shy or quiet around strangers.

Making a poor mouth – Crying poor, pleading poverty.

Making headway – Progress. To make headway on a sailing vessel is to make ground by sailing to windward.

Malagash – Peninsula on the Northumberland Strait in Cumberland County that is home to Jost Winery, Nova Scotia's largest wine producer of Nova Scotian grapes. The place name comes from the Mi'kmaq Malegaawach, meaning "place of games." See also Merigomish.

Malignant Cove – Antigonish County community named after a shipwreck. In 1774, HMS *Malignant* went down nearby and despite efforts by a number of locals to renamed the community Millburn, the old name has remained.

Man from Margaree – Moses Coady, born at North East Margaree in 1882. Coady became a well-known pioneer in the Canadian Co-operative Movement, establishing the United Maritime Fishermen Union and the Extension Department of St. Francis Xavier University.

Man trains – Trains that transported coal from the pit head to the ports of Cape Breton also carried the coal miners to and from the mines. On the Sydney and Louisbourg Railway line, miners were transported on "man trains" that were also known as hobos. These box cars were 50-foot in length with high windows, wooden benches, and in cold weather, a steam pipe from the locomotive's boiler pumped heat into the cars.

Maritime Rights – Political slogan of the 1920s citing federal indifference to the post World War I economic decline in the Maritimes. Another popular political slogan of the 1920s was "Justice for the Maritimes." See also Three Musketeers.

Marked gas – Gasoline taxes were established in the 1950s and in order to give fishermen and farmers a break on their transportation costs, they were exempted from the gasoline tax by being able to buy cheap coloured gas. This "marked gas" quickly became popular with many ordinary Nova Scotians who would secretly pay farmers and fishermen to buy extra fuel.

Maroons – Black Jamaicans who arrived as refugees in Halifax in 1796. The majority departed for Sierra Leone in 1800 but the Maroon legacy lived on in Nova Scotia.

Marry too far – To marry someone from far away.

Marshy Hope – The origin of this place name is interesting. According to Pictou County folklore, the community contained a marshland that was once farmed by pioneer Robert Mappel and despite disappointing results at agriculture, he always maintained hope the marshland would get better.

Mash – Moonshine.

Massacre Island – Small south shore island in Queens County where a local legend maintains that a French ship was wrecked and passengers killed by Mi'kmaq warriors. In Yarmouth County, there stands Murder Island near the Tusket Islands, and this island was once identified on a French map as Isle Massacre. Local legends suggest that the island is home to a number of dead individuals that were murdered in connection with treasure trove activities on Oak Island.

Masstown – Named to recognize a small Acadian church in the area where in September 2, 1755, Acadians were assembled to hear the news that they would be expelled from Acadia.

Maud – Canada's best-loved folk artist, Maud Lewis.

Mazing – Amazing.

Mckay Car – Nova Scotia's very own automobile, built by two carriage makers, Dan and Jack Mckay. The car factory operated in Kentville and later in Amherst, prior to World War I.

Measly – Tiny and not in the best of shape.

Meeting house – Old time church and community center.

Melter – Furnace worker at the Sydney steel plant.

Membertou – Mi'kmaq reserve in Sydney named in honour of the great Mi'kmaq Chief Membertou who died in 1610 at Port Royal at the ripe old age of one hundred years.

Merigomish – Pictou County coastal site that was named from the Mi'kmaq Mallegomichk, meaning "a site of merrymaking."

Mersey woods – Big tract of timber land along the south shore and inland that is owned or leased by the Bowater-Mersey Company of Queens County.

Mess shad – Phrase referred to dressed shad, fish that had been cut, split, deboned, and pickled in two-hundred pound barrels for export to the Boston markets.

Meteghan – Acadian community in Digby County. This place name can be traced back to the Mi'kmaq term Mitihikan, translated as "blue stones."

Metro – Halifax Regional Municipality where forty percent of the province's population resides.

Mi-Carême – Halloween-like festival celebrated by Acadians as a break from the fasting time over Lent. Gala event includes colourful costumes and much merriment especially around Chéticamp.

Michelin bill – Provincial labour law that ruled a workers' union could only be formed if a majority of company workers throughout the province vote in favour of the union. Individual factories could not unionize unless a majority of company workers in Nova Scotia agree. The bill effectively made a union at the Michelin Tire Company in Nova Scotia a very unlikely possibility.

Mickey priest – Catholic priest.

Middle of nowhere – Out in the sticks, close to being lost.

Mile house – During the stage coach era, public houses were established along the routes to and from Halifax. To mark the distance from the capital, the inns were given names such as Ten-Mile House and Eight Mile House.

Milk train – Prior to the automobile age, trains were everywhere and collecting milk from farmers was one task that trains did very effectively. For instances, outside Truro, the "milk train" would travel into town each morning at 8:00 am stopping at level crossings to collect milk from farmers. However, milk trains were not popular with all Nova Scotians because in the back of the train would be passenger cars slowly taking paying customers into town.

Minards: king of pain, rub it in – Advertising slogan for Minards Liniment, a powerful smelling rubbing ointment that was produced in Yarmouth and concocted to cure what ail's ye.

Mind like a sieve – No memory while mind like a trap-door means a sharp mind.

Mind – Recall, remember, as in "I mind the time last year…"

Mind the full moon in June – A clear night in June during a full moon can bring on a frost that can damage tender young plants.

Minudie – Cumberland County site on Chignecto Bay. The term comes from the Mi'kmaq word Munoode, meaning "sack" and historians think the name was coined because of the shape of the local marshland. Minudie was once called le champs élyseés in French colonial times and is still sometimes called Elysian Fields by locals.

Missing link – The old 22-mile railway gap between Digby and Annapolis Royal on the Halifax to Yarmouth rail line through the Annapolis Valley. The final link-up was completed in 1894 after the rail service between Digby and Annapolis Valley was established with the completion of bridges over Bear River, Moose River, and the Grand Joggin.

Mistake River – Digby County river that was mistaken once too often for the Sissiboo River and named accordingly.

Mixed marriage – Protestant-Catholic couple and if they wanted a big church wedding, the big question would be who was going over to the other side. See also, jumped the fence.

Monastery – Antigonish County community home to a monastery run by the Augustinian Fathers.

Money Pit – Nicknamed for Oak Island near Chester where for centuries, treasure seekers have worked in vain on one of the world's most notorious treasure mysteries.

Monkey birch – Stunted or discolored birch tree.

Monkey doddler – One who fathers an illegitimate child.

Mooch – To mooch off of someone is to bum free stuff without paying them back.

Moose heels – Old time moccasins also known as moose-shanks. They were made from the actual hide off the hind legs of a moose where the joint formed a natural heel.

Mooseland Trail – Early 20th century name for the inland route between Annapolis Royal and Liverpool where adventure tourists flocked to the big game hunting and fishing lodges around Kejimkujik.

Moose milk – Many different kinds of alcoholic concoctions but the one main ingredient in moose milk in Nova Scotia is rum.

Moose muffle – Hearty stew that includes moose meat taken from around the nose of a moose.

Moosewood – The striped maple also called moose maple because for some reason, moose seem to be attracted to browsing the tree. See also browse.

More out than in – Out of it, not fully functioning in the head.

Mosey along – To leave and carry on casually.

Mother Carey's chickens – From the Latin Mata Cara (Dear Mother or the Mother of God in French.) "Careys" are Storm-Petrels and fishermen regarded the arrival of this sea gull as warning of an incoming storm. Storm-Petrels were widely despised by light keepers for contaminating their drinking water collected in rain barrels.

Mother Coo – Ellen Coo was a feared woman who lived in Pictou County in the late 1800s. Mother Coo predicted a number of disasters especially coal mining explosions, and was considered a witch by many Nova Scotians.

Moxham's Castle – As the general manager of Sydney Steel, Arthur Moxham was one of the wealthiest men in Sydney and had his Scottish-style castle dismantled at his former home in Ohio and rebuilt on King's Road in Sydney where it stood for many years until destroyed by fire in the 1960s.

Mucking – Cape Breton mining term for working behind the coal cutter cleaning and shoveling out the duff (coal dust.) Mucking was tough work because the big coal cutter known as the Dosco miner used water when cutting coal and consequently the coal dust became heavy wet muck.

Mud Creek – Original New England Planter name for Wolfville. The name proved to be an embarrassment to the settlers and the village was renamed Wolfville in honour of the numerous DeWolf families that settled the area. However, a steam running through the town is still called Mud Creek.

Mud room – Back porch off the kitchen also called the sink room.

Muffled up – Heavily dressed up for winter weather.

Muggy weather – Oppressive sticky weather that comes in on a south wind.

Mug-up – Hot drink of tea, coffee, or a shot of rum.

Munit Haec Et Altera Vincit – Latin motto that appears on the escutcheon of Nova Scotia. It means "one defends and the other conquers" but oddly enough, there is no consensus as to the actual meaning of the phrase in relation to Nova Scotia's history.

Muskol – Local insect repellant developed by Col. Charlie Coll of Pictou County and first manufactured near Truro.

Mussel mud – Rich sea mud gathered from the coastal bays and harbours. Prized as fertilizer, the mud would be hauled up through the ice in winter and dumped on fields.

Muster up – This old military phrase now usually refers to fixing up a meal or a concoction of leftover food.

Muzzle loader – Rectangular wooden boxes open at one end and used as space-saving sleeping quarters in the old lumber camps around the Mersey woods.

My dream is out – Dream came true.

N

Nail her to the pin – Hold a vessel exactly on course.

Naked as a jay bird – Without a stitch of clothing on.

Nary – Not a one.

Nattering – Natter or nagging about something or ragging on it. Also, mumbling or talking indistinctly.

Necum Teuch – Eastern shore community near Moser River that comes from the Mi'kmaq term Noogoomkeak, meaning "fine beach sand."

Neighbourly – Friendly, helpful, and accommodating.

Never came over it – Never mentioned it.

Never darken a church door – Not religious and doesn't attend church.

New broom sweeps clean but an old one knows the corners best – Experience also has value.

New Light – Like the Great Awakening religious conversion in New England, the New Light movement swept through Nova Scotia in the late 1700s under the leadership of Horton preacher Henry Alline.

New Scotland – Nova Scotia.

Nictaux – Annapolis County community and this place name can be traced to the Mi'kmaq word Nittak, meaning "forks in a river."

Niddy-noddy – Gutless. Also, a sawney.

Nigh on time – Nigh is short for near. Left side of an ox team is the nigh-ox (right the off-ox) but the expression "nigh on time" means the "time is right." Also, as nigh as I can remember.

Nightingale – The beautiful song sung by the Hermit Thrush is so admired that the bird is sometimes called "the nightingale."

Nine ways to Sunday – Every which way to go.

Ninny – Fool.

Nip and tuck – Means touch and go, or hard to make ends meet.

Nipped in the bud – Taken care of before it got out of hand.

Nippers and wristers – Knitted fabric worn by fishermen at sea. Nippers were worn over the inside of the hand while handlining. Wristers were worn over the wrists to protect chafing and the onset of pingeons, painful sores that develop when skin rash and salt water come together over a long period of time.

Nippy – Cold weather.

Noddy – Local name for the Razorbill gull. Also called tinker.

Noggin – A quarter-pint wooden mug for drinking tea or hot-buttered rum. A noggin factory once stood at Greenwich near Wolfville and the community was then known as Noggin Corner.

No holds bared – All is fair. In wrestling matches, choke holds are often considered illegal and when a match is declared "no holds bared," literally anything goes.

No load to carry – Easy once you know how.

No-see-ums – Tiny flies that bit but you can't see them do it.

Nose to the grindstone – Hard working.

No skin off my nose – Doesn't affect me.

Not a word of a lie – The honest-to-goodness truth.

Not by near – Not nearly.

Not firing on all four cylinders – Person is not all there in the head. Also, not playing with a full deck, and three bricks short of a load.

Not her usual self – Something is not quite right with her.

Not too fussy – Don't like it as in "not too fussy about it."

Not worth a pinch of coonshit – Good for nothing.

Nova Scarcity – United Empire Loyalists' name for Nova Scotia after arriving in 1783 and finding the small colony poorly developed and thinly settled.

Nova Scotia needs a new direction – Provincial Liberal Party's 1970 campaign slogan that brought Gerald Regan, "the man for Nova Scotia" into power, defeating the Conservatives under the leadership of G.I. "Ike" Smith. Regan, due to his former radio sports announcer days, had been nicknamed "Gabby" and was considered brash but proved to be a formidable political opponent and held on to power until 1978.

Nova Scotian – Famous 19th century newspaper that blossomed under the editorship of Joseph Howe.

Nova Scotia turkey – Salt cod.

Novies and Yanks – Nicknames for Nova Scotians and New Englanders who fished side by side on the offshore fishing banks.

No way – Can't be done, no way in the world that can happen.

Now she's talking – Got the bugs out and everything is working well. Old nautical phrase for when a wooden sailing vessel is humming along with the familiar sound of sails, wind, and waves.

Now, sir, we know your city is something more than a shed on a wharf – Winston Churchill's famous remark to Halifax Mayor Lloyd during his visit to the city in 1943.

Nubbin – Green-horn or new at a job. Also can be used to describe something small or immature. Nubbin is not derogatory while nummie means stupid.

O

Oban – Community in Cape Breton near St. Peters. Oban in Gaelic means "little bay."

Obliging – Agreeable trait in a person.

Ocean Limited – CN passenger train that runs from Halifax to Montreal.

Offish – Someone who is stand offish or distant, unfriendly or overly quiet. Stand off is a nautical phase for steering clear.

Off island – Off and on. On shore-off shore, on land-off land. An islander on one of Nova Scotia's many offshore islands can have a different sense from mainlanders about what actually is meant by "off from on and on from off."

Old as Methuselah – According to Genesis 5:27, he lived to be 969 years old.

Old Barns – Community near Truro once settled by Acadians forced to abandon the area during the expulsion of 1755. When English pioneers arrived in the early 1760s, they encountered empty barns and named the site Old Barns.

Old dear – Term of affection in referring to an old person while "he's an old stick" means he is uptight and not well liked.

Old wife's tale – Not very reliable story.

Old Year's Night – Old Lunenburg term for New Year's Eve.

On a string – Having another girlfriend in another settlement and "stringing" her along.

On count – One of the various methods used to try and divide up the fishing catch among fishermen. The more preferable methods were by equal shares (or even shares) and by weight because as author Mike Parker points out in his book *Historic Lunenburg*, on count (or by-the-count) meant that the largest and most valuable fish were often thrown back overboard in order that the fishermen could fill their dory with smaller fish and receive a larger count.

One hundred percent – Full attention, no let up.

Only got one oar in the water – Not fully there in the head.

On my own hooks – Fishing phrase for independence, can do it on my own.

Onnery – Obstinate.

On the halves – Working for half the production while giving up the other half in exchange for services. Based on a loose 50-50 partnership where by one party would contribute labour on a fishing or lumbering expedition while the other partner would contribute equipment and transportation.

On the hustings – Going electioneering, running for public office.

On the make – Looking for opportunity. Can also mean on the sexual prowl.

On the round – Fish that hasn't been dressed.

On the shelf – Retired but if you are a retired mariner or without a ship, you are "on the beach."

Onto it – Special effort or attention paid to something. Also, into it.

Open-banded – Old-time name for single strand yarn produced on a spinning wheel. Two-ply yard was called double and twist, and three-ply, treble-the-three.

Orange and lemon Christmas – In the spring of 1894, the vessel *Bamboro* out of Sicily and bound for Boston, was wrecked off Shelburne County with a load of oranges and lemons. That Christmas, every child in the county received an orange and lemon in their Christmas stocking.

Order of Good Cheer – North America's first social club, established by Samuel de Champlain at Port Royal in 1606.

Orts and otts – Food scraps and leftovers fed to barnyard animals. See also, sinkswill.

Ostrea Lake – Community along the eastern shore once home to noted oyster grounds and named in recognition of the region's shellfish heritage.

O' the banks – Not the place where money is kept but the offshore fishing grounds –Georges, Browns, Western, Banquero, and Grand Banks.

Ottawa House – At Partridge Island on the Parrsboro shore stands a historic inn once owned by Sir Charles Tupper and so named due to the large number of prominent federal politicians entertained there.

Our future is here – Provincial Conservatives 1981 election slogan under the leadership of John Buchanan. The Conservatives went on to win 37 of the 52 seats.

Out of a clear blue sky – Unexpected, a total surprise.

Out on the Mira – Opening phrase of Allister MacGillivary's classic Cape Breton tune, *Song for the Mira.*

Outside fishing – Fishing offshore while "on the shore" means fishing inshore.

Out with the captain – South shore euphemism for gone drinking according to Lewis Poteet, author of *The South Shore Phrase Book.*

Ovens – The Ovens of Lunenburg County are ocean caves worn into steep coastal cliffs by relentless tides. Gold was first discovered at The Ovens in 1861.

Over a barrel – No way out. Expression is from the naval practise of flogging men over the gun barrel.

Overboard – Gone too far and ended up over the side and in the water. Getting in trouble by taking something too far.

Overfalls – Raging water running over sunken rocks.

Over his head – Over his head means that a person has taken on something bigger or more complicated than he is capable of undertaking.

Overman – On-site boss in a Cape Breton coal mine.

Owing to – Due to or because of. For example, "owing to the poor turnout, the meeting has been cancelled."

Owl – Freight train with one passenger car attached at the rear hauling a mixture of passengers and cargo. One who rode the owl "came on the freight."

Owly – Cranky, in a foul mood.

Own cousin – First cousin. Own son was a son that was not adopted.

Ox bells and fireflies – Traditional sounds of Nova Scotia in mid-summer.

Ox haul – Oxen pulling contest where teams would compete by hauling heavy drag-sleds weighted down with stones. Also called a pull with the most popular event known as the "hook-on-and-stay" competition.

P

Paid according to – Payment based on the value of the work, not by the hour.

Paint a boat green, not well received – A green boat in Nova Scotia is considered a bad omen.

Parade of concern – Black Friday occurred on October 13, 1967 when Hawker-Siddley and DOSCO announced that they were closing Sydney Steel, the economic engine of industrial Cape Breton. A citizens' protest march through the streets of Sydney was duped the "parade of concern."

Paradise – Annapolis County community named by French settlers and retained by English planters.

Parlour or the kitchen – Two sections of the old lobster pot that the lobster had the choice of entering. Either way the lobster gets trapped. Parlour in a house is the living room or more commonly called the front room.

Parrsboro shore – The scenic coastline along the north side of the Minas Channel between Five Islands and Cape Chignecto. This shore has also been called little Cape Breton because of the dramatic coastal cliffs.

Passed away – Died, went away to the "sweet by and by."

Passed his prime – Getting old, long in the jaw.

Passepec – Old name for Prospect.

Pasture pines – Pine trees growing out in open fields. They develop large branches that tend to be knotty and poorly valued by the lumber industry.

Patient waiter never loses – First radio wireless message transmitted by Guglielmo Marconi from Glace Bay to England in 1901.

Patti-pans – Cupcakes. Term comes from the French petit pains.

Pay for a dead horse – Pay for something that has already been used or discarded. See also flogging a dead horse.

Pay the decks – Nautical expression for sealing the decks with pitch. Boiling pitch would be poured into the deck seams to make them waterproof.

Peaked – Sickly looking.

Pea souper – Thick fog while a pea pod is a tiny boat.

Peelin' time – Stripping the bark off hardwood lumber. Often done in May and June. Peeling pulp wood was called spudding it.

Peepers – Small frogs also known as pink-winks along the south shore.

Peeps – The small or least sandpipers (including the Semipalmated Sandpiper) make a peeping sound and are known as peeps in Nova Scotia.

Peggy's Cove – Bruce Nunn, author of *History With a Twist*, was able to establish that the name Peggy's Cove came from a shipwreck victim Margaret (Peggy) Weaver who was rescued off the cove in the 19th century.

Pensioned off – Descriptive phrase to describe an old or weak bird that stays apart from the flock.

Pent road – Private road with a gate at the outset.

Perish – To die from exposure, either at sea or on land from extreme temperature.

Pesaquid Lake – Lake on the Avon River near Windsor. This area was once called Pisiquid by Acadians and the name comes from the Mi'kmaq meaning "tidal forks."

Pickpocket – Nickname for Shepherd's Purse, an edible wild plant that is also known as Mother's Heart.

Pictou – The place name for this town can be traced to the Mi'kmaq Piktook meaning "fire." A number of explanations are plausible for the origins of this name including burning ship sightings and naturally occurring fire from coal deposits.

Pier, The – Whitney Pier outside of Sydney, named after Henry Whitney of Boston who consolidated numerous independent coal mining operations and became the first president of the Dominion Coal Company in 1890.

Pie Social – Traditional food festival in the rural areas of Nova Scotia. According to Marie Nightingale in her book, *Out of Old Nova Scotia Kitchens*, "Each lady would bake her favourite pie and carefully pack it in a basket to share with the gentleman who 'won' her with the highest bid." These pie auctions were often the first step in courting rituals.

Pigeon hawk – The Merlin was once known as the Pigeon hawk since it resembled the now extinct Passenger pigeon while in flight.

Piggyback Railway – Nova Scotia's unique piggyback railway was first introduced in the 1850s on the government constructed Nova Scotia Railway between Windsor and Halifax. Stagecoaches and wagons could be winched onto railway flatcars and hauled into Halifax at incredibly low prices. The popular service was quickly over subscribed and then cancelled by railway officials.

Pile on the canvas – Putting more sail on a vessel. *Bluenose* skipper Angus Walters was notorious as a great sail carrier. The heavier the wind, the more he "piled on the canvas."

Pimpy one – Prissy, fussy.

Pines, The – Pines Hotel near Digby, one of Nova Scotia's more popular resorts. Originally built in 1892, the name was selected by owner Henry Churchill, not because of nearby pine trees but because Churchill liked the pleasing sound of the name and thought it would attract tourists to his resort.

Pink fish – Lobster.

Pinkie – A narrow stern vessel is a pink so that a pinkie schooner is a double-ended vessel. Once engines were installed in fishing vessels, the "double enders" were squared off at the stern to allow for the installation of the old "make and break" engines.

Pinks – Rhodora because when it is in bloom, the flowers produce a pink haze.

Pipe down – Be quiet. Naval expression since the last pipe each day signaled to the men to "pipe down."

Pissabed – Dandelion that was used as a natural diuretic.

Pissing in the wind – Doomed, stupid, no hope of succeeding.

Pissing the bed awake – Really stupid.

Pitch in – Helping out.

Pithead – The entrance to a coal mine.

Pitman – In olden days, hand saws were used exclusively and the pitman would stand under a log in a sawpit and saw the log.

Pit props – Timber stakes used to frame up coal mines. Also called poles.

Plaster board – Gypsum, a large industry in Nova Scotia especially in Hants and Victoria Counties.

Plastered – Drunk as in "I got plastered last night."

Played out – Tired.

Playing hooky – Skipping classes at school.

Pledge – To take the pledge was to abstain from all "intoxicating liquors." Years ago, a community-wide pledge would be organized by religious organizations and temperance societies around the New Year.

Plug – Logs caught up in one place on a river drive was known as a plug. If the entire log drive was plugged up, it was called a jam.

Plumb – To enlarger an expression as in "we plumb forgot about you."

Ply – To bend or shape something.

Pockwock Lake – Main water reservoir for the Halifax Regional Municipality near Mount Uniacke. The term comes from the Mi'kmaq word Pogwek and can be translated as "Smokey Lake."

Pogie – Unemployment Insurance now called employment benefits.

Point pull and be damned – Rough and windswept site near Victoria Beach at Digby Gut where according to Mike Parker in his book, *Historic Digby*, fishermen in the pre-motorized days of sails and row-boats, had to row and pull against the current to get out into the fishing grounds of the Bay of Fundy.

Pollywog – Tadpole.

Poly-asses – Small mattresses in bunk beds used in the old lumber camps.

Pomquet – Antigonish County coastal community that comes from the Mi'kmaq Popumkek, meaning "fine sandy beach."

Ponhook Lake – Queens County lake that can be translated from Mi'kmaq as "first lake in a chain of lakes."

Pool of still water – Place where one can have some peace and quiet.

Poor man's weather glass – The Pimpernel flower who's petals fold up just before rain.

Popple – The poplar tree.

Pop the question point blank – Having a frank, straightforward talk.

Portable soup – Solid stock of soup mixture much like the bouillon cube today that could be transported and used as the base for a new batch of soup. Also called glue and pocket soup.

Portapique – Community on Cobequid Bay that comes from the French word for porcupine.

Port Mouton – Queens County community named by the explorer Du Gua de Monts in 1604 after one of his sheep drowned during a landing.

Postmaster and road man – Two jobs that were always in jeopardy at election time.

Potatoes and point – Funny expression found in C. Russell Elliott's book *As the Twig Is Bent* about growing up in rural Nova Scotia. Hard up families in the depression would eat nothing but potatoes while all pointing to a tiny piece of meat in the center of the table.

Pot belly – Large gut. Also, a pot-belly stove was a cast-iron stove with a wide middle.

Pot calling the kettle black – Both are to blame.

Pot of Gold – Nova Scotia's very own brand of chocolates produced by the Moirs Chocolate Company.

Pounding – Threshing and treating something reckless such as "I pounded that truck into an early grave."

Pour – Measurement of liquor as in, the restaurant serves a good pour, meaning a generous glass of wine while a bad pour means a small amount of wine is served. Free pour means the bar is open and the cost is "on the house."

Poutine a Trou – This special Acadian desert "pudding with a hole" combines diced apples, raisins, cranberries, and pork fat with sugar and water and baked in a pastry shell.

Poutine râpée – A holiday Acadian dish of grated potato wrapped into a ball around a minced pork core.

Prairie Sailor – Inefficient sailor or rower.

Prayer handles – Small windows directly underneath eaves on homes that are quite common along the south shore.

Preacher gull – Nickname for the Great Black-backed Gull, the largest gull in the world. A number of explanations are often cited as to why this gull is called preacher or minister. The most likely comes from Robie Tufts who notes that as an adult, the "minister bird" features a black mantle that contrasts sharply with its bright white plumage.

Precious – A tiny amount as in a precious little. Also can refer to affection, as in calling a young child, "my precious."

Prefabs – World War II prefabricated houses that are still in use throughout the province.

Pretty near – Close but not there yet.

Pretty tough doing – Depression-era description of most people's living conditions.

Preventive Service – Special anti-bootleg force set up throughout Canada during the Prohibition era. A.T. Logan from Pictou Country ran Nova Scotia's "preventatives" and broke up many smuggling operations between 1929 and 1933.

Price busters – Costco Canada.

Prick – Dirty bastard.

Prig – Steal.

Prime berth – Fishing phrase for the very best location on the water to set traps.

Princes Lodge – In Rockingham on the Bedford Basin near Halifax there once stood the 18th century royal estate of Prince Edward, Duke of Kent. The lodge near the shore was a favourite retreat for the Prince and his companion Julie St. Laurent. All that remains today is the lodge, now known as Princes Lodge.

Proof of the pudding is in the eating – We'll only know in the end.

Proper thing – The fair thing to do.

Public wharf – Local wharfs throughout Nova Scotia that until quite recently were maintained by the federal government for the common use of the community.

Puckerstring – Drawstring.

Pugwash – Community on the Northumberland Strait that comes from the Mi'kmaq word Pagweak, meaning "shallow water."

Pulling my mouth – Putting words into my mouth or contorting my meaning.

Pull your dory up alongside anytime – Drop over to our house anytime.

Pull yourself up by your own bootstraps – Do it on my own, no help. Also, all by one's lonesome.

Pumpkin king – Windsor's famous giant pumpkin grower, Howard Dill.

Punishment soup – Marion Robertson notes in her book, *The Chestnut Pipe*, that sea duck soup is one of the toughest dishes to eat. She recommends the following recipe. Put the duck in the pot with the vegetables and water. Cook until the vegetables are well done. Lift the lip and let the duck fly away. Eat what is left.

Punkin eaters – Hollowed-out Halloween pumpkin faces with lights inside.

Pussy-tails – Cat-tails that grown around the edge of swamps.

Put down – Can mean a derogatory remark but most common use is "put away," as in, "we put down forty quarters of berries last summer."

Put in – To apply, as in, "I put in for the pension last week."

Put men on the fish – In order to be successful, an experienced banks fishing captain had to know where the fish were and his job as captain, besides sailing the vessel, was to be able to "put men on the fish."

Put off – To get upset as in, "I was put off by George last night."

Put on the kettle – Stay for tea, coffee, and even lunch. Also, boil the kettle.

Putter around – Doing little of anything.

Putting on the ear cups – According to writer Clary Croft in his book, *Nova Scotia Moments*, early radios were equipped with earphones and one needed to "put on the cups" in order to get a good reception.

Put to rights – Bring around, plan or prepare an action.

Put up and shut up – No complaining, accepting a bad situation.

Put your damper down – Damper on a wood stove controls the airflow and keeps smoke from filling the room. Putting your damper down means to keep things tight – under control.

PWA – Provincial Workmen's Association, first miner's association in North American that was secretly formed outside of Springhill in 1879.

Q

Quaffed – Guzzled, drank, or otherwise inhaled the liquid.

Quare ways – Queer ways, eccentric.

Quat – Bend down as in "when I squat down, my knee hurts."

Queer one – Since the pig was once considered bad luck by fishermen, it had numerous nicknames including hoodoo, Mr. Dennis, and in Shelburne County, fishermen often called a pig "the queer one."

Quiet man from Nova Scotia – Robert Stanfield, one of the province's most popular politicians, was known for his modest demeanor but earned the title "political master of the province."

Quiffy – Being "quiffy" means being snobby.

Quintal – Old unit of measurement for fish, 110 pounds of uncured fish or 100 pounds of cured fish.

Quoddy Harbour – Eastern shore community with a place name that is traceable to the Mi'kmaq Noodaakwade, meaning "seal hunting grounds."

R

Rabbit wood – Odds and ends that are "rabbited" together to create furniture.

Race for real sailors – This famous phrase was coined in 1920 when the owner of the *Halifax Herald*, William Dennis, announced the establishment of an annual International Fishermen's Race that would featured a race of fishing vessels manned by "real sailors." The *Bluenose* was launched the following year and quickly became "the pride of the fishing fleet."

Racket – Scheme or your line of work but also can be used to describe an outbreak of unwanted noise.

Rack – To search as in to "rack one's brain for the answer."

Rain bird – The Black-billed Cuckoo is believed by some to be predicting rain when it emits a strange calling sound, "coo-coo-coo."

Rainbow at night, sailor's delight, rainbow in morning, sailor's take warning – This weather saying can be traced to the Blandford Peninsular.

Raining cats and dogs – A lot of rain. One of Thomas C. Haliburton's many sayings.

Rainworms – Thirsty worms that are drawn up from the ground in anticipation of a coming downpour.

Rake – A little passenger rail car that had six seats and took twelve miners deep underground into the Cape Breton coal fields.

Rappie pie – Acadian meat and potato dish from southwestern Nova Scotia.

Rassling – Wrestling.

Rattle your socks – Real big deal.

Rattling Beach – Site on the Annapolis Basin near Digby where the sound of waves moving stones under water seem to account for the origins of this place name.

Reach for the top – Popular 1950s-era Maritime TV quiz show for school kids.

Read it in Rural Delivery – Country magazine published out of Queens County by Dirk van Loon.

Ready for paving – Clever provincial Conservative Party slogan that helped win the 1956 provincial election fought in part over the issue of road paving. Robert Stanfield became Premier of Nova Scotia defeating Liberal leader Henry Hicks in part by claming that Hicks was fighting for re-election by having his party "ready for paving."

Ready money – Depression-era phrase for actual cash as opposed to credit.

Red Army – Nickname for the Dexter Construction's gigantic fleet of road building vehicles, everything from massive earth moving vehicles to caterpillars.

Red Row – Company row housing in Sydney Mines. The 12 attached brick and wood units are the last remaining row of houses out of 11 such rows that once housed hundreds of miners and their families.

Reel – To reel them off means to talk fast, be able to list off a string of words or rhymes. This expression has nautical roots since sailing lines were often kept on reels in order to speed up their dispatch.

Rendez-vous – In the days of the press-gangs when finding sailors for ocean-going vessels was not always easy, a rendez-vous meant going on a mission to find sailing recruits.

Repeal – Popular slogan throughout Nova Scotia during the post Confederation-era when demands to repeal the act of Confederation and do away with the Dominion of Canada was most strong in Nova Scotia. Joe Howe was the most vocal advocate of the anti-Confederation movement.

Reserve Mines – Cape Breton mining community that was once "reserved" by the General Mining Association (who owned all provincial coal mining rights during much of the 19th century) for future mining.

Rhine of Nova Scotia – South side of Bear River near Digby with it's picturesque scenery and lush landscapes.

Rigamarole – Round about, convoled, and most certainly entangled.

Riggers – Workers who erect the rigging on sailing vessels.

Right on the bite – Got all the answers.

Right smart – Very smart. Right is often used as an intensifier. He was right keen on her, i.e., he liked her. Also, went right down for going down.

Rights River – As Margaret Harry points out in her article, *The Place Names of Nova Scotia*, this river in Antigonish County near Pleasant

Valley was not named to commemorate a dispute but in honour of a settler named Wright.

Rimrack – To search out, damage, and destroy.

Rinctum – Going off in a fury. Marion Robertson in her book *The Chestnut Pipe*, makes mention of an especially violent fit of rage called "rinctum diddy."

Ringer – A very good athlete, scratch golfer, or someone who is on top of his game.

Ring-me-up – Call me up on the telephone.

Ring-neck – Also known as ox-eye, the Semipalmated Plover is well known for locating its' nest on sand beaches.

Ring the woods – Hunting practice of spreading our in a circle to ensnare an animal.

Rita Joe – Whycocomagh Mi'kmaq poet who spent much of her life in Eskasoni writing poetry that reflects traditional Mi'kmaq culture.

Rita – Rita MacNeil, a Cape Breton icon along with the singing choir, Men of the Deeps.

Ritching round – Restless or hot to trot.

River drive – Sending logs down the river during the high water season each spring.

Roaring up – Charging up in a hurry.

Robin's snow – April snowfall that arrives after the robins appear. Snow is known as poor man's fertilizer because it holds moisture longer and melts slowly, allowing nutrients to fertilize farmer's fields.

Rob roy – Hastily built porch to shelter an outside door on a house.

Rock hound roundup – Annual fossil festival held each August at Parrsboro. In 1984, fossil collector Eldon George found the world's smallest dinosaur tracks at Wasson's Bluff.

Rockingstone – Site of a huge stone that rocks back and forward near the Kidston Lake area of Spryfield in Halifax.

Roll them up – Not the contest at Tim's but what a log team would do: roll up logs onto skids in a yard.

Roll-your-own – Cigarettes rolled from loose tobacco and also known as makings as opposed to tailor-made smokes, purchased in a store.

Rooster – Ventilator on a chimney.

Rooting – Looking around here and there for something.

Rosen up the bow – Let's play some music. Also, put the bow to the fiddle.

Rotten dirty – Not nice as in, "he treats her rotten dirty."

Roughage pile – Heap of waste lumber.

Round Church – St. George's Round Church in north end Halifax was constructed in 1800 and is considered the first Byzantine-style church built in British North America. Most of the wooden structure was destroyed during a tragic fire in 1994 but has been rebuilt.

Rouse up – To rush or quickly put together something as in, "let's rouse up a meal before we leave."

Rubber – Condom. Rubbers refers to knee length rubber boots.

Rubbing off the velvet – Moose antlers are covered certain times of the year in a mossy soft substance nicknamed velvet. During rutting season, browsing up against trees causes the velvet to rub off.

Rule – Cooking recipe.

Rummage – To search through a pile of items in order to find what you are looking for.

Running him up – Old trick at a county auction to get someone to bid too high on an item they really want by bidding against them. Yet if pushed too far, it could backfire because the fellows "running him up" could have it "dropped back on them."

Running his face – Buying on time, running a tab with the intention of paying up later.

Run – Swift flowing section of water. Also, going on a run can mean to take a trip by car or boat while running the roads means going on a tear.

Rustle up – Fix sometime up in a hurry.

Ryan Duffy's Stronghold – Bootleg liquor shop on Market Street in Halifax during Prohibition. The shop had steel doors and iron bars on the windows.

S

Sack suit – Quaint pre-World War I men's suit worn by townsmen on their best days usually with a tall, narrow brimmed bowler hat.

Sad – To be in sad shape means in bad condition.

Sail dragger – Too much sail for the vessel.

Saint John boat – *Princess of Acadia* ferry that crosses the Bay of Fundy between Digby and Saint John.

Saladin – Infamous piracy case that involved the vessel *Saladin*. The barque was discovered aground near Canso in 1844 and the crew was tried for murder in Halifax. Four seamen were hanged on the South Commons and as Thomas Raddall writes in *Halifax Warden of the North*, "the piracy case set all Halifax agog."

Salt box – Wooden two-storey house with a steep saddle roof resembling an 18th century salt box.

Salt fish, mutton and potatoes – What many Cape Bretoners lived on during the lean years according to author Tony MacKenzie in his book, *The Neighbours Are Watching*.

Salt horse and hard tack – Old 19th century nautical phrase for ship rations comprising salt beef (sometimes salt horse) and hard, dry biscuits.

Salting it away – Keeping something back for a rainy day. Until recently, much of Nova Scotia's fall harvest of vegetables as well as fish and meat would be salted and "put down" into cold storage in the cellar for eating during freeze up.

Salt marsh milk – Milk that stinks from cows eating too much salt water hay.

Samphire greens – Wild edible plant that grows around salt marshes and tidal flats. Real name is Glasswort but is also known as Saltwort.

Sand spits – Sand bars that appear between the shoreline and the ebb tide.

SAN – Nova Scotia Sanatorium for TB or "the consumption" that operated outside Kentville between 1904 and 1977. Once tuberculosis was eradicated in the 1970s, the provincial treatment center was closed.

Sapping – Intensifier as in "sapping wet."

Saw horse – Wooden apparatus that holds logs at waist level for sawing.

Saxby Gale – A massive hurricane that devastated the Fundy Bay area during the evening of October 4th, 1869, resulting in seventy-one deaths. The storm had been predicted by a British Naval officer, Lieutenant James Saxby, and turned out to be one of the greatest natural disasters to strike Maritime Canada.

Say it, don't spray it – Reaction to someone with a cold, sneezing and coughing.

Say nothing and be glad – You'll be glad later that you held your tongue. T.K. Pratt and Scott Burke, authors of *Prince Edward Island Sayings*, note a similar phrase popular on the island, "say nothing and saw wood."

Scad – A tiny bit while scads mean a large amount.

Scaling figures – Amount of logs harvested on a daily or weekly basis. A pile (brow) of logs would be measured by a tape or a scaler's rod, and this scale figure served as the basis for the logger's pay.

Scallop shucking – The delicate art of opening scallops, perhaps the most exquisite seafood in Nova Scotia.

Scantling – Small piece of lumber such as a stud, brace or tie. A scantling line in a sawmill would involve working with small timber pieces too tiny for boards or deals.

Scarce as leap year – Not plentiful.

Scarfing – In the old steel plant at Sydney, scarfing was one of the final steps in producing steel and involved taking flaws out of the steel.

Scarf – The first notch made by a tree chopper. The cut goes down on a slant and then straight across, and was known in the lumber woods as "the scarf."

Scaterie Island – This island is near Louisbourg and the name comes from the Basque word Escatarai, meaning "steep coastline."

Scattered – A scattered time means a rare time.

Schuss – Lunenburg County term for village idiot.

Scoffed – Seized or taken, not quite stolen but getting close because it was taken without permission but then again it may have been found. However, a scoff is a large meal.

Scoot sled – Sled with ski runners that could haul a portable mill in wintertime.

Scotched it – Put a stop to it.

Scot free – Got off without being punished, not even a slap on the wrist.

Scotian Gold – Annapolis Valley farmers cooperative and product marketing brand that became synonymous with Nova Scotia fruit and vegetables throughout the mid-1900s.

Scraggley – Sloppy looking.

Scraping the bottom of the barrel – Hard up, using the last scraps before your reserves are empty.

Scrawny – Thin and unhealthy.

Scrodger – South shore expression for an odd nautical assortment of iron bars, old crankshafts, rings and hooks, that would be welded together and lowered to the ocean bottom to snag old anchors and lost equipment. Scrod is a name of anything of poor quality.

Scrounder – Someone who searches for discarded or lost objects.

Scrub board – Old hand wash board.

Scrub – Playing scrub or pick-up baseball without teams mainly due to a lack of a full roster. Individual players rotate from batting to playing the field.

Scrub spruce – Stunted spruce trees that appear along the shoreline but can't really grow due to the salt water spray off the ocean. Also, cat spruce and mink spruce. Scrub pine is a common name for Jack Pine.

Scrunch – Crunch.

Scullywagger – Derogatory nickname for the sculpin fish because it is gross looking. To call someone a scullywagger is to call them down.

Scuttlebutt – Daily or on-going gossip. Origins of this term can be traced to the nautical world where the daily ship water rations were kept in the wooden "scuttlebutt" cask and sailors lining up to get water would exchange idle chitchat and hearsay.

Sea in your blood – Common phrase for those who choose a life at sea.

Sea manure – Seaweed or "sea dung" used to fertilize gardens along the coast. Sea punkin is often used in Digby County as a nickname for sea cucumber.

Sea parrot – Because of its parrot-like beak, the Atlantic Puffin is called sea parrot by fishermen in many parts of the province. Another name is parakeet.

Sea pigeon – The Black Guillemot, fairly common in Nova Scotia along the Atlantic coast.

Sea smoke – Fog that comes from cold air overtop warm water.

Seattle East – For a few years in the early 1990s, Halifax's vibrant pop music scene that included the talented rockers Sloan, was considered Canada's answer to Seattle's renowned grunge rock scene.

Seawater in her timbers – Water-logged vessel swollen from too many trips at sea.

Seaweed bird – The Ruddy Turnstone earns its nickname by feeding among the kelp at low tide.

Second Christmas Day – Boxing Day.

Second Sight – Someone with second sight is said to be able to see an event taking place even through they are not present.

Seine – Net for fishing that is hauled along or behind a boat.

Sell like stink – Real big seller.

Set down – Sit down. Also, set to is a brawl.

Set out the clothes – Hang clothes out to dry on a clothesline.

Sets – A number of lumber camps. Each camp was considered a set. If a lumber company had four sets in the woods that meant they had four separate lumber camps going at the same time.

Setter – Sawmill worker that operates the set-works (device on a sawmill carriage that would establish and maintain the thickness of the sawcut) in a sawmill operation.

Seven settlers, seven hills – According to Tom Sheppard in his book, *Historic Queens County*, the interior of Queens County was first settled by Europeans in the early 1800s when seven men, six Scots and one Irishmen, each chose a drumlin (small hill of fertile soil common in Lunenburg and Queens Counties) for their farm.

Sewn up – Taken care of. "All sewn up" means there is no more opportunity.

Shabang – The whole affair, everything.

Shachly – Slang tern for defective blocks once used by the hundreds on farms and dockyards. When combined with ropes, these wooden blocks could hoist and move most heavy objects.

Shack dwellers – Hermits, living off the grid. Shack yourself means living by yourself.

Shacking – Going fishing for hake or herring, in fact any fish but cod and halibut. Shack was any fish that fetched low prices on the wharf while cod and halibut were the most sought-after fish on the Atlantic coast.

Shag Harbour – The name Shag was derived from the old French name for the Double-crested Cormorant, once very abundant around this community.

Shake-hand soap – Nickname for the old surprise soap brand due to the picture on the package showing two people shaking hands (with clean hands of course.)

Shaker pans – A pan in an underground coal mine resembled a huge bread pan that held coal. A pan line was a number of pans bolted together that moved the coal from where it was loaded. According to author Rennie MacKenzie in his book *In the Pit*, a shaker pan was pulled along by a compressed-air, single piston engine that managed to shake the coal down the pan and into a conveyor belt.

Shannon and Chesapeake – Famous 1813 military engagement off Boston between H.M.S. *Shannon* and the American frigate *Chesapeake*. The victorious *Shannon* appeared in Halifax Harbour with the *Chesapeake* in tow.

Shape shingle – Special pattern-forming shingle.

Sharesmen – South shore phrase for men who work as fishermen and got paid by a share of the catch.

Sharp as a pin – Very smart, or quick. Also, sharp as a tack.

Shearin' time – Annual period when sheep were brought from far and wide to the shearing pen and given a haircut.

Sheep-shit tea – Clary Croft in his book *Nova Scotia Moments*, recalls growing up in Sherbrooke where the old folk remedy for curing measles, "nannie tea" was nicknamed sheep-shit tea since one of the indigents was sheep dung.

Sheila – Woman, term is Irish in origins.

Shellacking – Chewing someone out. Also, a beating.

She-shall-burn – How Shelburne got its' name according to historian Marion Robertson, citing an unhappy and rowdy settler who was forcibly escorted out of the harbour yelling back to those on shore "She-shall-burn, She-shall-burn." The name actually came from the Mi'kmaq Aogumkeagun, meaning "channel cut through a sand bar."

Shilly-shallying – Not serious, fooling around and being less than responsible.

Shin-dig – Party, rumpus affair.

Shined up – Got loaded on moonshine.

Shinimicas River – Cumberland County river that empties into the Northumberland Strait at Northport and means "shining waters" in the Mi'kmaq language.

Ship's Railway – Henry Ketchum's great scheme to build a railway system across the Isthmus of Chignecto in order to haul ships from the Bay of Fundy to the Northumberland Strait. He almost succeeded but went bankrupt after completing most of the project.

Ship-shape – Tidy up, to have everything squared away and in top working order.

Ship's husband – Agent for the ship's owner who sailed on board.

Ship's knees – Rare but naturally curved or crooked pieces of trees that were used to support the vessel's structure. Dory knees were similar pieces of wood but in the 1880s, Shelburne dory builder Issac Crowell began to mass-produce dories by creating the dory clip – two pieces of straight wood that were joined together by a metal clip to support the dory's skeleton.

Shit-faced – Drunk.

Shit fit – A tantrum, to get angry.

Shithawk – South shore term for seagull.

Shit or get off the pot – Make a decision.

Shooks and shingles – Shooks are wooden pieces either tops, sides, or ends, and are produced in sets that are assembled into boxes or barrels. Shingles are thin wedge-like pieces of wood, asphalt, or slate used as the outside finish for a building.

Shoot – Narrow and fast section of running water.

Shoot the breeze – Talking casually about this or that.

Shore captain – Tug boat captain or one who hugs the shore. Shoreman is a business partner in a fishing operation who docsn't go to sea.

Shore lark – Nickname for the Horned Lark that spends much of its' time along the shore in late fall and early winter.

Short spring, early autumn – Epitaph in the Pictou Cemetery marking the early death of the son of Rev. Norman MacLeod.

Shotfirer – The coal miner with the job of setting off the blasting power.

Show a leg – Mariner's phrase for get up, rise and shine.

Shrouds – Ropes on a vessel that extends down from the masthead to the vessel's hull.

Shrub – An old naval drink served at militia reviews composed of rum, peppermint, and aniseed.

Shubenacadie Sam – Woodchuck at the wildlife park that suddenly becomes very important on groundhog day. Will he see his shadow?

Shubenacadie – This place name comes from the Mi'kmaq and means "where groundnuts grow." Groundnut is similar to the sweet pea, grows in damp soil, and produces a sweet tuber popular with the Mi'kmaq.

Shuck. – Take away, remove a shell from an oyster or clam.

Shy – Short of money as in "are you a bit shy this week?"

Sick abed in the woodbox – Too sick to do anything but lay in the wood-pile.

Sick bread – Plain toast to feed a sick person.

Sidehill farm – Farms located on the slopes of North and South Mountains in the Annapolis Valley.

Sidney – Nova Scotia's most talented hockey player, Sidney Crosby.

Sight for sore eyes – I haven't seen you in awhile. Also, sight to behold.

Silly old coot – Expression comes from the odd habits of the American Coot. This bird dives, bobs, and splashes around at random, and is considered senseless and silly.

Silver Dart – Famous Cape Breton pioneer airplane that flew the first flight in Canada over the Bras d'Or Lake at Baddeck in 1909.

Silver thaw – Snow followed by freezing rain and turning everything into a hard gleam.

Singalong Jubilee – Produced for CBC TV by Manny Pittson and featuring a popular cast and crew including Bill Langstroth, Catherine McKinnon, and Anne Murray, Singalong Jubilee became a household name throughout the Maritimes during the 1960s.

Sink swill – Table scraps that are fed to farm animals.

Sit down and tuck in – Please stay for supper.

Six of one, half a dozen of the other – May seem different but it's the same thing in the end.

Sixty-four pieces – Standard number of shares that went into the financing of a sailing vessel.

Size of a barn door – Really big, wide as a barn door.

Skidding – Dragging logs in the winter over frozen ground.

Skipper – Captain, master of a ship.

Skunk cabbage – This early flowering edible plant does stink but its roots can be roasted and eaten.

Skunk Spruce – Nickname for White Spruce, one of the province's more common softwood trees.

Slabs – Waste pieces of lumber that are cast off in the sawing process.

Slack cupboard – Place in the forecastle of a fishing vessel where the cook kept lunch food and snacks. A "lunch up" was a snack between meals and while on board a fishing vessel, the crew would be free to access the cupboard most times of the day.

Slack – Loose.

Slag – Waste discharge from Sydney Steel.

Slap jacks – Rubber boots cut off as low rubbers.

Slapped in – Job was done haphazardly.

Slew – Quite a lot as in a slew of cars.

Slingload – Load of wood usually about half a cord that would be place into a sling contraption and hoisted or winched on to a deck of a ship.

Slink – Poor quality salmon that has recently spawn and is weak.

Slippery side up – After a rain the ground is wet and slippery.

Sloop – South shore nickname for one ox. Also called smiler, sheely, shafter, and jolly.

Slosh – To slosh about on the water is to be thrown around by the force of the waves.

Slow and lazy – Nickname for the Sydney and Louisbourg Railway that first opened in the 1890s to transport coal from the pitheads to the ice-free port of Louisbourg during wintertime. The S & L line was discontinued in 1968.

Slow as an ox – Slow yes but reliable.

Slow pokes – Herring dish that has been de-boned, rolled in flour and butter, and slowly baked in the oven. Also called potted herring.

Sluice – An open top water trough made of wood and designed to transport water over distance. The sluice gate is the vertical slide gate that controls the water flow.

Slush fund – Secret stash. Phrase comes from the nautical world where cooks often kept a secret hoard of fat known as slush that would be jealously guarded since ship's crew were always on the lookout for grease in order to lubricate the ship's equipment and rigging.

Smackers – Dollars, money. Also called spondulance.

Smart cookie – Someone who is clever.

Smidgen – A tiny slice is a smidgen.

Smithie – Blacksmith.

Smoke house – A wooden structure where fish are traditionally smoked over a bed of wood chips and sawdust. The word lox refers to almost any kind of smoked salmon. One of the best known firms, J. Willy Krauch & Sons, has been smoking fish in Tangier since 1956.

Smoke rises in the air, good weather, smoke falls, there's rain – Weather lore.

Smokey – Cape Smokey at Ingonish. From a distance, the cliffs look like smoke clouds.

Smokin' oakum – Exclamation, similar to Holy cow!

Smugglers Cove – Digby County community with numerous caves that faced out to sea and were used extensively during Prohibition.

SMU – St. Mary's University.

Smutched – Covered or smothered over.

Snag rubbers – Rubber boots worn by fishermen.

Snakevine – Tiny edible evergreen plant that produces berries in the fall and is better known as partridge berry.

Snapped up – Drunk.

Sniffing bowl – For relief from a stuffed head, a bowl of hot brandy or rum would be prepared and sniffed.

Sniggering – Gossiping.

Snig road – Temporary road built by swampers to haul logs from a cutting area to a brow (logpile.) A snig horse and crew would work the road and go sniggin.'

Snippy – To get snippy is to get uppity and act superior.

Snotlocker – Nose.

Snouted it – Old lumber expression for the work timberjacks did in clearing bush, cutting trails, and limbing fallen logs so that the yarding horse wouldn't get hung up in the tree falls around a chopping.

Snowbanker – According to Lewis Poteet in his *South Shore Phrase Book*, a snowbanker is a big awkward American car that performs poorly on snowy roads and would sometimes hits snow banks. Also called a Yank tank.

Snow bird – The Snow Bunting tends to arrive in Nova Scotia in late fall usually in time for the season's first snowfall. Juncos can also be called snowbirds due to their pale plumage in winter.

Snub – To "snub" him is to cut him off or ignore him in an almost brutal fashion. Term in the nautical tradition means to cut off a ship's movement.

Snuff – Up to snuff is in good working order so not up to snuff would be below par.

Soaked – Wet but also can mean cheated as in "he really soaked you on that one."

Sober Island – Clear-header island off Sheet Harbour on the eastern shore.

Sobeys bag – Plastic shopping bag first popularized in the Maritimes by Sobeys.

So cheap they could skin a louse and tan the hide – Person is pretty tight.

Social bees – Traditional get-togethers in rural parts of Nova Scotia featuring a theme, for example, a sewing bee or quilting do. See also Frolic.

So hungry I could eat a horse – Starving.

Solomon gundy – Salt herring that has been marinated in spices and vinegar.

Some good – Some good as in "very good." Some is often used in Nova Scotia as an intensifier and so is right. Thus "right some good" would be double some good. The phrase some good can be traced back to southwestern England. See also Right smart.

Son-before-the-Father – Since Coltsfoot, an edible wild plant, produces its blossoms before the leaves appear, it has the more common name of Son-before-the-Father.

Sooky baby – Crybaby and a sook.

So tall he had to bend for the doorways – Tall man.

So tight he squeaks – Penny-pincher.

So tight that not a chink of daylight showed through – That's chinking (closing the gaps in a log house) it close. See also stogin.'

South wind brings rain – Weather prediction from the south shore.

Sou'wester – Unique-looking fishermen's rain hat made from cotton and soaked in linseed oil.

Spanking brand new – Right out of the box, never before used.

Spare yourself short – Yarmouth County expression for causing yourself to be short, not keeping enough for yourself.

Sparrow hawk – According to Robie Tufts, the American Kestrel is our most common hawk and its' nickname sparrow hawk is a bit unfair since it feeds mainly on insects.

Spa Springs – Annapolis Valley's famous spring water site at Wilmot.

Spell – Period of time.

Spic and span – New and in mint condition. A new vessel was all "spic and span" since all spikes (spic) and timbers (span) were bright and shinny.

Spigot and bung holes – Large and small holes in a molasses barrel.

Spills – Evergreen needles. Known as sprills on the Miramichi in New Brunswick.

Spin-it-out – Staying late at someone's place when they are ready to go to bed. Spit-it-out is a phrase used to encourage someone having trouble communicating.

Spleeny – Hypersensitive, grouchy.

Splitterman – Sawmill employee who separates the sawn boards after the log has passed through the saw. Splitting wood means to chop the round pieces apart to burn better and splitting fish means to cut the fish through the center and take out the backbone.

Spook farm – The strange spook-house fires of 1922 at Caledonia Mills in Antigonish County, is one of the most famous mysteries or criminal cases of arson in the history of Nova Scotia. The poltergeistic happenings at Black John MacDonald's farmhouse captured headlines worldwide.

Spoonbill duck – The Northern Shoveler has an odd shaped bill, longer than the bird's head and broader at the end. Hence its name and nickname.

Spot-rump – Nickname for the Short-billed Dowitcher, a common spring bird in eastern Canada.

Spotter – Person who spies for swordfish from the mast of a vessel. The sticker is the one who throws the harpoon at the fish.

Spouter – Old nickname for a whaling vessel.

Spray – World famous sailing sloop built and sailed by Nova Scotian Joshua Slocum. Slocum was the first person to circumnavigate the globe single-handedly.

Spring burn – Traditional burn off of old growth in fields during the first dry spell each spring.

Spruce beer – Old time drink in Nova Scotia that may have originated with the Mi'kmaq and improved upon by the Acadians who added yeast and molasses. The basic recipe calls for sugar, yeast, vanilla, spruce extract, and boiling water.

Spruced up – Make over, a clean-up that improves the situation.

Spry as a grasshopper – Agile.

Squatted – Living somewhere on the sly, without having permission or ownership of the place.

Squawker – Nickname for a siren-type of radio apparatus that could break into radio broadcasts throughout Nova Scotia during World War II. The squawker was used often in the Halifax area to warn citizens of wartime emergencies and could emit both long and short blasts of offensive wailing sounds.

Spudge – Poke or stir up.

Squirmers – Eels.

Stabfart – One who constantly interrupts a speaker.

Staddles – Wooden platforms on the Fundy marshland that allowed cut marsh hay to stay dry during high tide.

Stake-driver – The American Bittern is a shore bird that has the remarkable ability to blend in well with its surroundings. It produces an odd sound that some claim resembles driving a stake into wet ground.

Stand on – Continue sailing along the same course.

Stand up for – Best man at a wedding.

Star of the Sea – Name for a 1930s Terrance Bay recovery project developed by the Sisters of Charity. A downturn in the fishery had left the community on the brink of starvation and with the help of the charity group, a handcraft program featuring weaving and woodwork was instituted, and the community was able to sell their hand crafted products under the "star of the sea" banner.

Stave mill – Mill that makes staves, thin pieces of wood placed edge to edge to produce barrels.

Stayhole – Underground coal mining term for a small hole in the coal made to brace six-foot timber support straps inserted into the coal face. This attempt to create a support system for the coal roof was called "legging the face" according to author Rennie MacKenzie in his book, *That Bloody Cape Breton Coal.*

Steaker – Fish large enough to be cut into grilling steaks rather than fillets.

Steaming – Going forward as in steaming along the railway line.

Stemmer – Cape Breton term for a beggar, one who panhandles on the street for change. In the acclaimed Cape Breton novel, *A Forest for Calum*, author Frank Macdonald writes, "Jonny Logan was a more familiar figure stemming money in front of the liquor store." A broom handle used to ram blasting powder into a hole in an underground coal mine was also called a stemmer.

Stem the tide – Over coming the effects of the in-coming tidal action by sailing through.

Stepping the masts – After a sailing vessel is launched, the next step is to install the masts. Stepping of the masts involves inserting the masts and supporting them with rigging including wire cables called stays (forestays and shrouds.) This task was one of the most delicate operations of shipbuilding and *Bluenose* Captain Angus Walters always maintained that the secret to the success of *Bluenose* was that it had been "stepped mathematically perfect."

Sternfull – A good catch as in a sternfull of cod.

Stewiacke – Colchester County community with a name that can be loosely traced to the Mi'kmaq Esiktaweak, meaning "slowing winding along."

Stick a fellow – South shore expression for spearing a fish.

Stick in the mud – Negative person. Expression comes from the writing of T.C. Haliburton.

Sticky – Hot and humid. Early days of a Nova Scotia summer.

Stile – Popular lookoff park overlooking Gaspereau Valley on Ridge Road above Wolfville.

Stinkplant – A special fish plant that renders fish waste such as heads and tails into fishmeal. Very smelly place.

Stinkwagon – Nickname for early automobiles that were powered by crude gas engines.

Stinkweed – Common name for Pennycress, a fairly large edible weed.

Stitch in time saves nine – One of many wise saying first coined by T.C. Haliburton.

Stocking up for a rainy day – Getting provisions now because it may be scarce later on.

Stog'em – To stog is to fill or "chink" moss between logs in a log cabin in order to insulate and tighten up the building. To build a log cabin was to log'em and stog'em.

Stogged up – Filled up to the max.

Stomp the cabbage – South shore expression for making sauerkraut.

Stone boat – Sled with runners designed for ox to haul rocks off fields.

Store-boughten – Bought or purchased as opposed to home-made.

Stormstayed – Prevented from traveling due to bad weather.

Straight out – Going straight out is going hard at it for an extended period of time.

Strapping – Big and strong as in "he's a strapping young lad."

Straw boss – Worker not really in charge.

Strawny – South shore phrase for understand or figure out.

Strike out – To head out for somewhere.

Striker – A striker worked with a teamster and looked after repairing the roads and keeping the horses fed and watered.

Stroke oar – The pacing-setting oar.

Strong run on – Usually used in relation to the sea and meaning a big tide or wind is creating a high sea.

Stuffed to the rafters – Full, too much to eat. Also, stuffed to the guppers.

Stuffing – A person's insides as in "he knocked the stuffing out of me."

Stumpage – Acres or hectares of standing timber. Cruising for timber involved looking over the timber in order to try and calculate the amount of board feet that could be cut from a stand.

Stunned – Not on the ball, a bit slow.

Subchasers and gunboats – Motley motor flotilla of vessels that comprised Halifax's anti-submarine fleet that protected the harbour during World War I.

Sugar pear – Nickname for Indian Pear, an edible plant that grows in the woodlands throughout the province.

Suit of sails – A compete set of sails for a vessel.

Sulphur and molasses – Old time spring ritual similar to today's flu shot. Widely regarded as a preventive measure given especially to children, dry sulphur was mixed with molasses and one teaspoon would be swallowed daily for up to one week. Sulphur is a common bleaching agent and regardless of the health implications of fumigating the human body, the smell was deadly, and young people would not go courting until the "cure season" was over.

Sun dog in the south, storm approaching, sun dog in the west, fine weather to come – Lunenburg County weather lore.

Sunshiny shower won't last an hour – Old weather wisdom. Also, rain before seven stops at eleven.

Sun will still shine – No matter the problem, life will go on.

Superficial foot – Board measure of one foot of lumber, one square foot, one inch thick.

Superline – Early chain of gasoline stations set up under the Super Service banner throughout Nova Scotia in the late 1920s. Under F.C. Manning's leadership, the company operated twenty-five gas stations throughout the province.

Super – Prohibition term for an on-board smuggler's representative known as the super or supercargo, who would give the captain last-minute instructions on where and when the contraband would be off-loaded or picked up.

Swale – Fertile lowland usually along a river that gets flooded most spring seasons and produces good quality hay. Also known as an intervale.

Swallow the anchor – Retire from the sea-going life.

Swampers – Men who built temporary winter roads for hauling lumber by clearing brush, tamping down the earth, and sometimes pouring water over the road to create a hard frozen surface. See also snouted it.

Swamp potato – Nickname for Arrowhead, an edible wild plant that grows in wet areas and produces tubers resembling potatoes. Delicious when cooked.

Swamp Spruce – Common name for Black Spruce since it can thrive in bogs and damp soil.

Swarm of bees in June is worth a silver spoon – Bees in late spring or early summer are considered good luck for the coming growing season.

Sweating bullets – Very worry.

Sweating like a hen hauling wood – Working hard, maybe going nowhere. Also, running around like a chicken with its' head cut off.

Sweat out – Final stage of the old three-week fish curing process when the last amounts of moisture were dried out of the fish. Soft (wet) and hard (dry) cures indicated remaining amounts of moisture in a marketable fish.

Sweep – Long bladed-oar used for steering a vessel. A sweep is also a long pole with a pivot that holds a cooking pot over an open fire.

Swig – A small drink.

Swipers – Legendary one-piece hockey sticks made near Antigonish by craftsman Charlie Young in the early 1900s. The swiper stick was made from hardwood with the blade formed naturally out of the tree root.

Switchel – In haying time in Nova Scotia, a jug of haymaker's switchel was carried to the field and stored in a cool place in order to quench a thirst during the heat of the day. The drink contained water, molasses, brown sugar, vinegar, and ginger.

Switzerland of Nova Scotia – Promotional name in the tourist industry for the community of Bear River with its' steep slopes rising up from the riverbanks.

Swonked – Tired from all the work, swamped.

SYSCO – Sydney Steel Corporation.

T

Taken aback – Surprised, and not pleasantly so. Expression comes from the nautical phrase sails aback, a sudden wind that quickly shifts the sails and the sailing direction of the vessel.

Taken down a peg – To lose a notch in one's pride or social standing. The phrase derives from the British navy where commanders had individual flags but could only fly them a certain height based on rank.

Take the town apart – Popular expression among military personal in Halifax during World War II due to boredom, crowded conditions, and shabby treatment by Haligonians. This threat became a reality during V-day celebrations in May of 1945 after liquor stores were closed.

Taking turns sitting up – Sharing staying up overnight with a sick person.

Talk is cheap but fish is scarce – Lunenburg County expression for all talk and no action. Also from the Annapolis Valley – talk is cheap but it takes money to buy a farm.

Tallahassee affair – The setting was Halifax Harbour during the Civil War era. British Halifax was anti-Union and when the Confederate raider *Tallahassee* was chased into Halifax by two Union cruisers, the city was in an uproar. While the Union cruisers waited off Chebucto Head, *Tallahassee* was guided out to the safety of open water through the narrow Eastern Passage channel by local pilot Jock Fleming.

Tallywagger – Pecker or penis. Tallywack is a scoundrel.

Tancook Whaler – Unique fore-and-aft schooner-rigged fishing vessel that first appeared around Mahone Bay near Tancook Island in the late 1800s. The word Tancook comes from the Mi'kmaq k'tanook, meaning "out to sea."

Tangled up – Getting involved, expression can convey negative connotations for example, "getting tangled up with the wrong crowd."

Tar-paper shack – Living in a real dive.

Tar ponds – One of the worst industrial dumpsites in Canada near Sydney where toxic waste run off from the steel plant has collected for almost one hundred years.

Tarred and feathered – Old time punishment. Also, lay on the rawhide.

Tatamgouche – Community on the Northumberland Strait in Colchester County. The place name comes from the Mi'kmaq Takumegooch and a number of meanings are possible including William Ganong's interpretation "the place that lies across" and Mi'kmaq scholar Silas Rand's version, "barred across the entrance by sand."

Tatties'n herrin' – Boiled salt herring with potatoes, a popular fishermen's meal. Before cooking salt herring, the fish would be soaked in fresh water overnight in order to remove some of the intense salt taste.

Tattle tongue – Telling on someone, a snitch.

Tea-caddy – Small wooden boxes that tea or "tay" came in up until the Second World War. Expensive tea caddies could be quite exquisitely carved and were often made from mahogany or walnut.

Teacher-bird – According to Robie Tufts, the Ovenbird is nicknamed the teacher-bird due to its loud and distinctive sound commonly interpreted as "teacher-teacher-teacher."

Teamboat – The first ferry launched by the Halifax Steam Boat Company occurred in 1816. A true steamboat proved too expensive for the company and so they built a horseboat (powered by horses instead of steam) and named it "teamboat."

Teaser – Failing to escape a British warship, the American privateer *Young Teaser* is set on fire and destroyed by her crew in Mahone Bay in 1813. The name Teaser became part of the folklore of the south shore.

Teetotaller – Drinks no alcohol, only tea and soft drinks.

Tell a skit – Tell a joke.

Tell tale – A sign, signal or warning as in "there wasn't a tell tale that a storm was coming in."

Tempest in a teapot – Much ado about nothing, simply a bump on a log.

Tending out – Two crews would be organized for the annual river log drive. The "tending out crew" would go with the logs to try and keep them running. A second "rear" crew would come up behind and do the dirty work, breaking the jams, and fetching the stray logs. In New Brunswick log drives, the rear crew did what was referred to as "the sacking."

Tending round – Seen at the same place several times as in "she's tending round here a lot."

Ten dollars a thousand and fifty for a thousand – Before the government scale came into the woods, to calculate a thousand feet, some buyers would claim that it took fifty logs to make it and they would only pay ten dollars a thousand at roadside for the best pine. The seller would try and counter that the buyer was damn cheap and even dishonest.

Tent dweller cruise – Famous ten-day adventure canoe trip through the wilds of southwestern Nova Scotia as celebrated in Alfred Bigelow Paine's delightful 1908 book, *The Tent Dwellers*.

Terns – Three-masted schooners.

Terry's Creek – Old name for Port Williams.

That I didn't know – South shore habit of starting a sentence with "that."

That takes the cake – Wins the prize for the biggest, best, but also can be the worst.

That takes the wind out of your sails – Crushing blow.

There'll be more progress with Stanfield – Provincial Conservative Party campaign slogan during the 1960 election. Robert Stanfield proved a popular Premier and again defeated the Liberals under Henry Hicks.

The thing of it is – The point of it is...

The time tonight – Big social event is happening tonight.

The wood ain't growin' yet that'll beat Bluenose – Captain Angus Walters' favourite saying.

They were nailin' cod to the masts – Old saying out of Lunenburg for a big catch during the heyday of the banks fishery. In the 1880s, Lunenburg County had almost 200 salt bank schooners working the banks and 500 fishermen employed.

Thin as a rake – Too thin to cast a shadow.

Thing-a-ma-jig – Refers to anything hard to remember or rarely used. Ding-a-ma-doggy is a similar expression in Shelburne County. Also doflicker, and a similar term that may have originated in Cape Breton is queermajigger

Thinking tacks – Sharp. To have your thinking tacks on is to be able to come up with good ideas.

Thistle-bird – Also known as the wild canary bird, the American Goldfinch spends much of its day feeding on thistle seeds.

Thorns'em – Real pain or thorn in the side, a bother.

Those days – Them times. Auger days. Nostalgic memories of the good old days.

Three A's in her name – At one time it was considered good luck for a saltbank vessel to have three A's in her name and a number of fishing schooners reflected this superstition including *Alcala*, *Delawana*, *Mahaska*, and *Canadia*.

Three Fathom Harbour – Eastern shore community with a three-fathom deep harbour.

Three Musketeers – Premiers Baxter of New Brunswick, Stewart of Prince Edward Island, and Rhodes of Nova Scotia who joined forces in 1925 to champion the Maritime Rights bandwagon in lobbying Ottawa for a better economic deal.

Three sheets to the wind – Drunk. Sheets are ropes that control sails and more than two sets of sheets in the wind is considered sloppy sailing.

Three squares – Three square meals a day. The phrase square meal is thought to have come from the era of the wooden ships when sailors without plates would be served dinner on a square piece of wood.

Through the back door – Getting in by going around regular channels.

Thrumcap Shoal – Dangerous rocky ledge off Herring Cove at the entrance to Halifax Harbour. In 1797, HMS *Tribune* collided with the shoal and went down in a southeast gale within sight of cliffs now named Tribune Head.

Thunder struck – Dumb founded, unable to think straight.

Ticket – Captain's ticket refers to the certification papers authorizing that person to assume command of a ship. Master's ticket is the right to become first mate of a vessel.

Tickle – Small and hazardous channel in Richmond County at Lennox Passage.

Ticklish – Tricky, not a straight forward affair.

T'ick o' fog – Fog is thick.

Tide has turned – Campaign slogan of provincial Conservative Party in 1949 under the new leadership of Robert Stanfield. Against Stanfield's conservatives ran Angus L. Macdonald's liberals with their slogan, "All's well with Angus L." Macdonald's Liberal Party retained 28 of the 37 seats.

Tide over – Lay low until conditions are favourable. Expression comes from mariners content to avoid sailing on an incoming tide.

Tidnish – Cumberland County place name with Mi'kmaq origins. Mtagunich has been translated as "paddle."

Tidy fortune – Cleared and free with plenty of money left over from the deal.

Tie-eye – Commotion or disturbance. Origins of this phrase can be traced to the south shore according to author Lewis Poteet.

Tierce – Unit of measure for molasses, halfway between a barrel and a puncheon, and measuring approximately two barrels while a puncheon measured four barrels.

Tight as a drum – Snug and secure.

Timberdoodle – Nickname for the American Woodcock.

Timber-drogher – Name for an old ship that was confined to hauling rough timber to Britain. Drogher is a derogatory term and many sailors who worked these decrepit vessels called them coffins ships since many disappeared at sea.

Time just drug and drug – Time went slow, dragged on.

Time to climb the wooden stairs – Time for children to go upstairs to bed. Adults, it's time to hit the sack.

Tim Horton Jesus – For some time in the late 1980s, the mysterious figure of Jesus on a wall at Tim Horton's in Bras d'Or brought hundreds of Cape Bretoners each day to witness the image.

Tim's – Tim Hortons where a double-double can be heard constantly.

Tin Cow – Famous old Reindeer brand of condensed can milk first produced by the Truro Condensed Milk and Canning Company in 1883.

Tin ear – Unmusical.

Tingling – Sensation that can serve as a precursor to something more serious, for example, "he had a tingling sensation just prior to the stroke."

Tinkers – Undersize fish or shell fish. Also, useless bits of junk.

Tipsy – Slightly drunk and loosing one's balance.

Tits up – Lying on your back, incapacitated, perhaps drunk or otherwise out of commission.

Tizzy – In a tizzy, upset and maybe a bit flustered.

To a T – Accurate. To know him "to a T" is to know him well.

To a watery grave – Died at sea.

Tobeatic – Large wilderness preserve in southwestern Nova Scotia. Tobeatic comes from the Mi'kmaq word Toobeadoogook but the precise meaning of the term is unclear.

To beat the band – Hard at it as in, "the snow was coming down hard, to beat the band."

Toddy – Small glass of rum.

Told him right to his face – Frank, forthright, and honest.

Toller – Nova Scotia's official dog, the Duck Tolling Retriever, originally bred and trained in the Yarmouth area of the province.

Toll grain – Most farmers in Nova Scotia did not own grist mills and would have local mills processed their wheat and grain in exchange for a percentage of the flour, usually 10-15 percent. The volume that remained with the grist mill was called the toll grain.

To make do – Settle for a little rather than nothing. Also to do, and to do without.

Tomfoolery – Nonsense.

Tommy cod – Young cod fish.

Tongue lashing – Balled out as in, "he got a real tongue lashing over that last infraction."

Tonnage – The weight of cargo that a vessel is considered able to carry. This could be calculated for wooden vessels by multiplying the length by the beam by the depth divided by a ton allowance.

Ton timber – Old time measurement for export timber. A ton would comprise fifty cubic feet of rough logs or forty feet of hewn (squared) timber.

Too big for his breeches – Acting bigger or smarter than he is.

Took a fright – Got scared.

Took their good-looking time about it – Dilly-dally around and didn't get it done on time.

Too many cooks spoil the broth – Too much and too many means overdone.

Top dresser – Manure spreader.

Top off the catch – On the way back from fishing on the Grand Banks, and if her hole was not completely full, a Nova Scotian saltbanker might dip over to fish off Sable Island and "top off the catch."

Tore the house down – Had a big party.

Tote team – Horse and wagon team that hauled supplies along a tote-road through the woods to a lumber camp. Toter was the hauler who drove the tote team and was also know as a teamster.

To the gills – Drunk, so full of liquor, he was full up "to the gills."

Touch and go – Delicate operation. In the book *Salty Dog Talk*, authors Bill Beavis and Richard McCloskey explain the nautical origins of this expression. Coastal sailing vessels in Britain rarely took sounding of the depths along inland rivers and would instead "touch" the bottom before "going" forward.

Town bicycle – Town whore.

Trailer Park Boys – Popular cable TV program (x-rated) about a greasy but loveable group of misfits shot in an actual trailer park near Cole Harbour.

Tramp the mow – Before the use of haying machines, hay was loaded by pitch fork on to the hay wagon. The job of children would be to "tramp the mow," pack down the hay so that a full load could get to the barn without tipping over. Once in the barn, children would play "tumble and roll" in the soft, fresh hay.

Trapper – Coal mining term for the worker with the job of opening a door underground to let the coal cars through. The door had to be closed quickly to trap the air and not allow it to leak out.

Treenail – Large wooden nail for securing planks and beams, and called a "trunnel" by shipwrights.

Tree run – Valley apples sold ahead of harvest on a "tree run" basis. As opposed to consignment, apples were sold at a firm (but discounted) price ahead of time and all apples that were produced on a tree would become the property of the buyer.

Trip – Cape Breton mining term for a underground coal train. Each car in a trip or train would contain a three-ton box and each trip would contain numerous boxes, some full of coal and some empty.

Trooper – To work hard and for a long time is to operate "like a trooper."

Trouble-man – Mechanics at the Sydney steel plant were called the trouble-men since their jobs involved fixing any equipment that went down.

Try cakes – Tiny cakes baked in order to test a recipe.

Tuckered – Tired.

Tugger – Cape Breton mining term for a winching machine that haul heavy loads and equipment underground.

Turn a blind eye – Pretend to not see for a larger good. Origin of this phrase can be trace to Nelson and the early 1800s. While in battle, Nelson turned his actual blind eye to the command signal to back off the attack and ended up defeating the enemy.

Turnip knurls – Scraggy. A face can sometime be described as resembling a turnip knurl.

Turnip – Nickname for a gentlemen's thick gold watch worn in his vest pocket and attached to a buttonhole in his vest by an equally heavy chain.

Turn of the tide – Ebb tide, slack water, or between the tides, when the water is essentially at a standstill.

Turn up – Crank up as in, turn up the heat in here.

Twaddle – Such nonsense.

Tweendecker – Square-rigged vessels between one and two thousand tons built along the Fundy shore. Hantsport alone produced almost one hundred such vessels.

25th, The – World War I Regiment made up of Nova Scotians. The 25th Battalion was part of the Canadian Expeditionary Force that served overseas from 1914 to 1918.

Twit – Clueless.

Two-four – Case of twenty four beer.

U

Udder – Other.

Umpteen – The umpteen time means so many times that it is beyond counting.

UMW – United Mine Workers' union.

Under the weather – Feeling off, not quite sick but definitely less than normal. Also, feeling weedy.

Underway – Pregnant.

University of the air – Informative and well-regarded CJFX radio program produced by the faculty at St. FX University in Antigonish beginning in the mid-1940s.

Unshrinables – Stanfield's famous shrink-proof underwear completed with the trap door backseat. The underwear was first developed during the days of the Klondike Gold Rush and sold as Stanfield's Unshrinkable Underwear. Sometimes also called "unspeakables" due to the prickliness of the all-wool material that did not breath.

Upalong – Up and over, or up and away from the Nova Scotia shoreline.

Up in back – Intensifier for in back, meaning farther back than simply "in back."

Uplanders – Old name for foxberries in Lunenburg County.

Upper Canada – Few people from Ontario or Quebec recognized this expression but it is still well used in the Maritimes.

Up the creek – In a tight situation. Also, up the creek without a paddle.

Up the ladder – Old, getting up the ladder is getting on in years.

Up to no good – Bad intentions.

Usige Ban Falls – Waterfalls in Victoria County on the Baddeck River. Translation from the Gaelic is "white water."

V

Valley – Annapolis Valley.

Valley's Johnny Appleseed – Apple grower Charles Prescott developed a number of unique apple varsities at his Annapolis Valley estate near Starrs Point.

W

Wackelass – To get in the way or underfoot.

Wad – Lots as in, "a wad of cash."

Wag – Waegwoltic Club in the south end of Halifax on the North West Arm. Name comes from the Mi'kmaq and means "end of the deep bay."

Wait on you hand and foot – Mother to daughter at lunch time: "Serve yourself dear, I'm not waiting on you hand and foot."

Waldeckers – German mercenaries who fought in the American Revolution and settled in Nova Scotia with the Loyalists in 1783. The mercenaries came from the Principality of Waldeck and the name can be traced to a fortified castle in the area.

Walking boss – Not the top boss in charge of the whole operation but the working boss who manages the timber stands and yards.

Wandering in his mind – Senile, suffering from memory loss.

Wants it buttered on both sides – Wants the impossible, both ways.

Warden of the North – Rudyard Kipling's great ode to Halifax: "Into the mist my guardian prows put forth, behind the mist my virgin ramparts lie; The Warden of the Honour of the North, Sleepless and veiled am I."

Warmest waters north of the Carolinas – Northumberland Strait.

Warming closet – Warming compartment or second oven on a cookstove.

Warn out – Prior to the era of the mechanical snow plough, each community in Nova Scotia was assigned a snow warden who would "warn out" all able bodied men after a snow storm to shovel snow and clear the public streets. The warden had the power to fine anyone who fail to show up at the warn out.

Washabuck – Community (includes North, Centre, and Lower) in Victoria County on the Bras d'Or Lake. The name is derived from the Mi'kmaq and means "a jut of land between a river and lake."

Wash your face off – Wash the dirt off your face. Also, dry your hands off.

Watering cart – Hauling timber out of the woods was difficult in the winter during heavy snow but next to impossible when no snow was on the ground. But a watering cart would be used to freeze over the road thus allowing a sled to haul logs out to the yards.

Waterworks – Trouble with your waterworks means you pisser isn't working right.

Way to go – Good work, great job.

Weasel – Sleazy.

Weather-breeder – Day that brings in a storm. Time when the storm is being "cooked up."

Weatherman is calling for rain – "Calling" is a holdover from older times when community elders, religious leaders, and weather experts would pray for much-need rain or sunshine.

We bloom amid the snow – Motto of the Nova Scotia Philanthropic Society describing the activity of the province's official floral emblem, the Mayflower.

Wedge up, knock down dogs – Final words on launch day when a newly constructed vessel would be freed from her fetters (dog clamps,) slid down the ways, and proudly entered the water.

Wed the garden – Weed the garden.

Wee waw – Zig-zag, walk in an awkward fashion.

Weighted anchor, set sail – To begin a sailing voyage.

Weir – A long tall fish trap made out of trees and brush erected on the Fundy marsh flats at low tide. Fish are then trapped inside the weir at high tide and scooped out after the tide has ebbed.

Went all haywire – Didn't work out, went every which way but straight.

Went trimming after them – Went running after them.

Were you born in a barn – Where are your manners?

West Novas – West Nova Scotia Regiment, the senior provincial regiment that fought overseas during World War II. Three other local fighting regiments were North Nova Scotia Highlanders, Cape Breton Highlanders, and Princess Louise Fusiliers.

Wet your whistle – Have a drink.

Whack – A large amount as in a whack of fish. Whacked up is to divide up according to who earned what. However, a fair whack would be a reasonable amount. A one time, a "whack" meant a sailor's food allowance.

Whale bird – The Red Phalarope sea bird is known to feed on the same plankton as baleen whales.

What – Finish a sentence with a what: "Ain't it hot today what."

What's your father's name – The start of many conversations among strangers in Nova Scotia.

Wheelhouse – Driver's seat.

Wheelin' sawdust – Tough job at a saw mill that entailed moving sawdust away from the saws.

When cats are frisky, a storm is brewing – Weather prediction.

When she's payin' – When things are working right. In the book *Woodchips and Beans*, author Mike Parker quotes an old-timer who worker many a log drives: "The boss come along. I said, 'You caught us standing here loafin.' He said, 'You know something? When you're standin' on the side of the river here and the logs are goin', that's when she's payin'."

Whiff – Trace, odour, small piece. A castoff whiff could be a seafood appetizer in some upscale Nova Scotia restaurants.

Whip-handle tree – Famous old elm tree in Upper Stewiacke. The story goes that pioneer farmer Samuel Fisher was finished ploughing his field one day about 1800 and stuck a switch into the ground he had been using to guide his oxen. The next spring he found leaves growing from the small branch and left it to grow into a might elm he called the whip-handle tree. The old giant elm was finally cut down in 1985.

Whipping post – Old time community site where public punishment would be dished out after a sentence was handed down.

Whipsaw – Up and down saw that required two men to operate, one above the log and one below.

Whisky and fight and stay out all night – Lumber camp tradition at break-up time.

White fleet – Portuguese deep-sea fishing fleet that featured white hulls and light coloured sails. They used North Sydney as their annual refuelling port.

Whitewashed Yankee – Nova Scotian by birth and American by adoption.

White-wings – Nickname for the Willet, a large shorebird that is quite common to Nova Scotia during the summer.

Whopper – Big tale, most likely a lie.

Whycocomagh – Inverness community that comes from the Mi'kmaq Wakogumaak, meaning "end of the bay."

Wide as the day is long – Big body on that one.

Wide berth – To steer clear of.

Widow maker – The bowspirit on a sailing vessel and many sailors were knocked to sea attempting to carry the bottom of a sail forward. The knockabout schooner was developed in New England to replace the dangerous bowspirit and became quite popular in Nova Scotia.

Widow's watch – Small enclosed site on a roof or a protruding upstairs window that faces the sea. The watch area allowed an anxious wife with a husband at sea to scan the ocean for an approaching sail. Also called widow's walk.

Willy nilly – Piecemeal, still not together with pieces scattered all over.

Wind in the east, fish will bite the least – Old fishermen's verse. Wind is in the south, bait will fall right in the fish's mouth. Wind is in the west, fishing will be the best. And when wind is in the north, never should a fisherman venture forth.

Wind is hauling – Weather is clearing.

Wind is in – Coming in from the sea and usually meaning bad weather.

Wind is off – Coming off the land and bringing fine weather.

Window party – Breaking windows.

Wingin – Complaining and fussing.

Wire birch – Common name for the Grey birch, a small tree used for fuel, barrel hoops, and spool wood.

Witch's tree – Mountain ash. Pieces of wood whittled from this tree were once considered by many superstitious folk to be good luck in keeping witches away.

Withe-stick – Springy stick with a sharp end use to hurl green apples.

Wolfed it – Gobbled it down.

Wong'n box – The big box or storage shed in a lumber camp held supplies and valuable items such as tobacco, hardware, dry goods, and extra clothes. Also called the wangan in Ontario and New Brunswick. Author Mike Parker in his book *Woodchip and Beans*, notes that in Nova Scotia, the wong'n box was also known as the van.

Won hands-down – Won the match fair and square, without question.

Won't wear it – Not able to take the abuse. Wear ship for a mariner is to tack by turning her stern through the wind rather than her bow due to rough conditions. In extreme situations, this is impossible, and the ship "wouldn't wear it."

Woodpecker mill – Not a serious, full-time saw mill but an operation that produces a little lumber from time to time.

Wouldn't say shit for a shovel full – Prim and proper.

Wracking – Salvaging a shipwreck. If a fisherman were offered the job of salvaging the cargo on a wreck, the salvaging company would subcontract the fisherman to be the wracker, and offered one half of the cargo as payment. This would be called "half-clear" work. The cargo would be referred to as the "pickings."

Wreck havoc – To create chaos and destruction. Also, mollyhawking.

Wrens – Women's Royal Naval Service (WRNS) was commonly known as Wrens and in Canada as WRCNS, constituting non-combat female military personal. During World War II, groups of Wrens were very common on the Halifax waterfront.

Wringin' wet outside – Very damp and you could get soakin' wet to your behind.

Wrong-way Stanfield – Liberal Party nickname for Robert Stanfield in the 1953 provincial election pitting Stanfield against veteran Premier Angus L. Macdonald. The Conservatives countered with "twenty's plenty" citing the fact that the Liberals had been in power in the province for a full twenty years. Liberals managed to hang on to victory and took 23 of the 37 seats.

Wrote a good hand – His hand writing was good.

X

X – St. Francis Xavier University.

Y

Yaffle – Chew. Farm yard animals are known to "yaffle" off half the vegetable tops in a garden if they get loose for more than a few minutes. Yaffle up can also mean to gather up a pile.

Yarding – Deer and moose yard up in periods of heavy snow by tramping down paths so they can move about in the deep snow. Also, yarding in a timber operation meant hauling logs out of the woods to a "yard."

Yarmouth Beauty – Prominent brand name for hand-rolled cigars produced by the Yarmouth Cigar Company in the early 1900s. L.J. Roy owned the cigar factory on Brown Street in Yarmouth where cigars were rolled by hand.

Yaw – To go off course on a sailing voyage due to a high surging sea.

Year of the big snowfalls – In 1905, Nova Scotia, especially the central region of the province, got hit with record amounts of snowfall throughout the winter.

Year without summer – In 1815, the Indonesian volcano Tamboro erupted sending huge amounts of dust, sulphur, and ash into the upper atmosphere. The next summer was dark and cold throughout eastern

Canada with crop failures, frost, and snow throughout the summer months.

Yellow hammer – Nickname for the Yellow-shafted Flicker due to the sound it makes hammering on trees.

Yellow Rocket – Edible wild plant also known as Yellow Cress and Spring Cress but has the official name of Wintercress. It is one of the earliest spring plants to appear in Nova Scotia.

Yinkyank – Local Cape Sable Island dialect that was spoken by settlers who immigrated to Nova Scotia from the Cape Cod region of New England.

Yodeling cowboy – Entertainer Wilf Carter left Nova Scotia with his distinctive yodeling sound to seek fame and fortune in the United States where he became popular as Montana Slim.

Yoke up – Hitch up a pair of oxen with a yoke. Many parts of the world use bow yokes that fit on the neck but Nova Scotia is known for its head-yoking tradition. Two yoke of oxen would be two pairs. Yoking would be breaking in an ox to learn to wear a yoke.

You better would – You better do it.

You can no more steer a pig than a hurricane – Country wisdom.

You can't get blood from a stone – Saying of Sam Slick, fictional character of writer T.C. Haliburton.

You couldn't cut it with a knife – Tough as leather, food was uneatable.

You don't make fish on Sunday – Long before the Sunday shopping controversy, working on Sunday was considered a no-no, and fish plants and flake sheds did not produce fish on the Sabbath.

You get the full weight buying from us – Old marketing slogan popularized by the Eureka Corn and Feed Mills in Liverpool around 1900.

Yunder – Yonder. Off yonder is somewhere else, over yonder is tomorrow, and up yonder is heaven.

Bibliography

A B Sea A Loose-Footed Lexicon
Jack Lagan, Sheridan House

The Birds of Nova Scotia
Robie Tufts, Nimbus Publishing

Centre of the World at the Edge of a Continent, Cultural Studies of Cape Breton Island
Edited by Carol Corbin and Judith A. Rolls, Cape Breton University Press

The Chestnut Pipe
Marion Robertson, Nimbus Publishing

The Clockmaker The Saying and Doings of Samuel Slick of Slickville
Thomas Chandler Haliburton, McClelland & Stewart

Da Mudder Tung
Glen Gray, Microtext Publishing

Down in Nova Scotia
Clara Dennis, Ryerson Press

The English Language in Nova Scotia
Edited by Lilian Falk & Margaret Harry, Roseway Publishing

Ethnicity and the German Descendants of Lunenburg County
Laurie Lacey, St. Mary's University

Folklore of Lunenburg County
Helen Creighton, McGraw-Hill Ryerson

Forest For Calum
Frank Macdonald, Cape Breton University Press

Historic Digby
Mike Parker, Nimbus Publishing

Historic Lunenburg
Mike Parker, Nimbus Publishing

Historic Queens County
Tom Sheppard, Nimbus Publishing

New Brunswick Phrase Book
Dan Soucoup, Pottersfield Press

Nova Scotia Book of Everything
John MacIntyre and Martha Walls, MacIntyre Purcell Publishing

Nova Scotia Moments
Clary Croft, Nimbus Publishing

Old Time Travel in Nova Scotia
Edith Mosher, Lancelot Press

Ox Bells and Fireflies
Ernest Buckler, McClelland and Stewart

Prince Edward island Sayings
T.K. Pratt and Scott Burke, University of Toronto Press

Sailing Alone Around the World
Captain Joshua Slocum, Sheridan House

Salty Dog Talk
Bill Beavis & Richard McCloskey, Adlard Coles Nautical

So Much Weather
Gary Saunders, Nimbus Publishing

South Shore Phrase Book
Lewis Poteet, Lancelot Press

That Bloody Cape Breton Coal
Rennie MacKenzie, Breton Books

Woodchips and Beans
Mike Parker, Nimbus Publishing

Politics of Nova Scotia 1896-1988
J. Murray Beck, Four East Publications